de
s

Other books by Mike Riddell

Fiction
The Insatiable Moon

Non-fiction
Godzone
Threshold of the Future
alt.spirit@metro.m3
God's Home Page

deep
stuff

Mike
Riddell

A LION BOOK

Text copyright © 1999 Mike Riddell

The author asserts the moral right
to be identified as the author of this work

Published by
Lion Publishing
Sandy Lane West, Oxford, England
www.lion-publishing.co.uk
ISBN 0 7459 4041 2

First edition 1999
10 9 8 7 6 5 4 3 2 1 0

Acknowledgments
Sylvia Plath, 'Lady Lazarus', reproduced by
permission of Faber and Faber Ltd.

A catalogue record for this book is available
from the British Library

Typeset in 12.5/15 Venetian 301
Printed and bound in Finland

**For Polly,
and her amazing
technicolor quest**

Chapter One

Life is what happens
when you're busy
making other plans.

John Lennon

John is having one of his blank spots. He becomes aware of the silence. There are four pairs of eyes watching him. He's in a strange room. One of the curtains has come away from its track at the end. Through the window he can see a tree and a brick wall. There's a pot plant which needs watering. Somewhere here there must be a clue to the meaning of it all.

He looks around at the faces, and exhales.

'Sorry?'

Tasha narrows her eyes. 'I just wanted to know if you had any strange habits,' she says. 'Train-spotting, sacrificing black rabbits, doing drugs; that sort of thing.' She leans forward.

'I pray,' says John, his eyes still slightly glazed.

'On what?' asks Quentin.

'Uh, no – I mean as in meditate sort of thing.'

'Oh god,' sighs Quentin in a patently irreligious cry. 'You're not a bloody Bible-banger, are you?'

John wants to get up and water the pot plant. And it wouldn't take a minute to fix that curtain.

'I don't think so,' he says.

Sometimes the most
important thing in a
whole day is the rest
we take between two
deep breaths, or the
turning inwards in
prayer for five
short minutes.

Etty Hillesum

'This praying,' Tasha rejoins the interrogation, 'it's not going to affect us, is it? You do it in private? Not like wanting grace at mealtimes or anything?'

'In private, definitely. And only with consenting deities.'

'Leave him alone,' says Siobhàn. Her nose stud glistens in a ray of sunlight. 'I meditate, and it's never bothered any of you, has it?' She smiles at John in solidarity. 'And Claire goes to church sometimes. Don't you, Claire?'

The long-limbed woman adopting the lotus position on the floor looks up at the sound of her name. 'Pardon?' she asks.

'Granted,' declares Tasha. 'Look, I'm happy with whatever you're into as long as you keep it to yourself and it doesn't put the hens off their laying. I'd be more worried if he was a vegetarian. You're not, are you?'

'Carnivorous through and through. I consume dead animals on a daily basis,' John reveals.

'Gross me out,' mutters Claire.

'And you're a New Zealander?'

'Undeniably,' the newcomer concedes.

'Well John, I'm prepared to give it a go,' offers Tasha. 'What do the rest of you think?'

'Just pretend I'm not here,' says John.

Being the most recent arrival entails the smallest room in the house. This is ancient lore and not to be questioned. Generation after generation has ordained that it be so. Best not to tamper with the order of the universe.

So it is that John finally concedes that there is not enough wall space for all his pictures. The 'Be Just Where You Are' poster is returned to its tube and laid to rest in the wardrobe. But Kurt grimaces at him from above the bed. And there is

I have no doubt that it is a part of the destiny of the human race, in its gradual improvement, to leave off eating animals, as surely as the savage tribes have left off eating each other when they came in contact with the more civilized.

Henry Thoreau

room on the small table for his clock, the candle and an ashtray. Symbols of a life.

There is a window, even if it's on the dark side of the house. And from his first-floor vantage point he can view these things: the side of the house next door; a tree with spreading branches; and (by lying on the bed) a fragment of sky. The sky today is dirty blue. The leaves on the tree are lime green, though a few have begun to brown around the edges. The wall of the house next door is regulation magnolia.

He is unpacking his life once again. Arranging his meagre possessions in a new way in a new place. Making this space his space, as much as is possible. As he has done too many times before. You leave bits of yourself behind. Some things you can't take with you. What would it be like to put two stones next to each other, and come back years later knowing they remained in the same place?

I recreate myself every time I do this. Each new combination of elements marks a new persona. But who is the person behind the masks? Is there anyone there at all?

Nicotine asks no questions, but tells no lies. John enjoys the sweet smell of tobacco as he constructs the cigarette.

She has become wary of the coffee plunger. When she went to the emergency department, they told her it was so common that they had a name for it – 'Bodum arm'. She was sure it would scar, but it healed well. Still and all, Siobhàn takes

8

it very slowly and carefully when pushing down the plunger. Treating it as hostile.

Who was it now – Brigid? Yes, Brigid, who had the conspiracy theory about coffee. Ever wondered, she would ask, why it never tastes as good as it used to? It's because of stuff they're putting in the water. Worse than fluoride. Top secret. True. It makes people passive. Compliant. Look at people's eyes next time you're on the bus.

Siobhàn takes a big hit, nonetheless. Caffeine jump start. Who could live without it? Synapses clocking in progressively.

John lumbers through the door, absentmindedly scratching at his groin. Siobhàn pretends not to notice. He has a fleck of white shaving cream under one ear.

'Morning,' he announces.

It is not her normal practice to converse before the second cup, but she makes an exception for the new boy.

'Settled in all right?' she enquires, feigning interest.

'Possibly,' he ventures. 'Let you know in a fortnight.'

John opens and shuts cupboard doors, in an uncoordinated fashion. He is clearly looking for something. Aren't we all? thinks Siobhàn. He can play the helpless male as much as he likes. I'm not his bloody mother.

'Ah,' he congratulates himself, discovering the bread in the fridge. He tries to appear nonchalant while scanning for the toaster. Siobhàn has her head down. The newspaper is a place to hide. John is becoming more confident as he assembles the equipment for breakfast. He begins to hum. A riff from the Pogues which has taken up residence in the part of his brain used for idling.

Siobhàn narrows her eyes and tightens her lips. Turns a page with menace. All to no avail. 'For fook's sake,' she complains.

'Sorry?' John is all little-boy innocence.

'I'm not too good in the morning, John. D'you think you could lose the humming, if that's what it is?' Already she is beginning to regret her encouragement of this new flatmate. I'm getting too old for this. A nice little place on my own.

'Right, yes, sorry. Just filling in the space, you know? I'll stop. Ah, marmalade?'

'Top cupboard on your right.'

John returns to his rituals. The tune keeps playing in his head, but he manages to keep it there. He carries his plate of toast and mug of coffee to the table, carefully sitting at the other end from Siobhàn. He munches the toast noisily. Trying to read the back of the paper. Looks out the window whenever she turns a page.

Closing her eyes in pain, Siobhàn capitulates. She lays the paper down.

'Good coffee,' says John, brightly.

Oh god, she thinks. Deliver me from mornings.

The cursor blinks vacantly. Quentin looks at it, waiting for it to move. It stares him out. He feels his whole being sliding into resonance with the

> I don't generally feel anything until noon, then it's time for my nap.
>
> Bob Hope

pulsating emptiness. Waiting for something to arise.

A writer writes. A dreamer dreams. This morning there is nothing coming. Dark shapes moving slowly in the depths, but not a word breaking the surface.

He taps his fingers on the keyboard in annoyance. Purses his lips. Looks around the room for inspiration. A picture of the White Duke stares back at him. Is that mockery in his eyes? Or boredom?

You're a fraud, he tells himself. You're not a writer's toerag. A poser, who sometimes strings words together but never has them published. Over his shoulder the black spectres of the void are calling to him. Wanting to enfold him in the numbing arms of depression. Soothe him with their cracked voices.

Quentin the unfortunate. The Don Quixote of the writers' group, tilting at the Ultimate Story. Apologizing that he couldn't get started this week...

The cursor continues its commentary.

'Bollocks!'

'Up yer bum!'

'Look,' says John, 'it wouldn't matter if you cut the benefit in half – there's just no reason for them to get involved. No motivation, no sense of participation, no skills to work the system.'

'How bloody patronizing can you get? That's exactly what I'd expect from a social worker. We're

Writing comes more easily if you have something to say.
Sholem Asch

I always do the first line well, but I have trouble doing the others.
Molière

talking about people like you and me, who've got the same choices we have. I'm bog fookin' Oirish, for chrissake; my father was a brickie. No one handed anything to me on a plate. I made my own way. No excuses, no sympathy.' Siobhàn bangs her empty mug on the table for emphasis.

Quentin stands in the doorway in silent wonder. Siobhàn's always passionate, but not normally at this time of the morning, and not with comparative strangers.

'Getting to know each other, are we?' he asks while pouring a coffee.

'We're having a discussion,' explains Siobhàn, eyes gleaming. 'John here is your original bleeding-heart liberal social worker, who wants to protect the poor from the ravages of the heartless capitalists.'

'And Siobhàn thinks that the whole world can be fixed with education. Typical individualist right-wing propaganda,' retorts John. 'You've bought the whole programme, haven't you? No problems that a bit of entrepreneurial intellect can't solve.'

They stare at each other across the length of the table. Quentin sits down, smirking.

'Well, children. Don't let me interrupt you. Just try to keep the blood off the newspaper will you? I haven't read it yet.'

It's never *quite* the same as the photos. She has the magazine propped up against the mirror, and is trying to follow the five-step instructions for creating 'Lips that Glow in the Light'. Still, she decides, pressing her lips together, it's not bad.

Claire requires considerable time to fashion herself each day. There's so much to it. Discerning the mood of the day, and thinking about how to respond to it. Mulling over clothes and colour combinations while in the shower. The hair. And then creating the face. It's like having to paint a portrait before breakfast every day. And the shoes, of course. That's the one that often stumps her and makes her late. No matter how many she buys, there's never the right pair to make her look *perfect*.

She stands this way and that. Steps back from the mirror and draws near to it slowly. Examining it all with the eye of the professional. Readjusting strands of hair. Picking at non-existent threads on her blouse.

'I don't know why you bother,' Tasha often told her. 'It's just a dress shop.' But of course it wasn't *just* a dress shop. It was Pink Angel. Tasha wouldn't understand. And bothering isn't something you can *choose* not to do – you either do or you don't. I do, Claire tells herself. Bother.

There's a lot of noise coming from the kitchen.

'Oh, come on, Quentin, you can't be serious!' Siobhàn is laughing without humour. 'Why the hell should I go out to work all day to support you with my taxes just because you declare yourself to be a sodding artist?'

'So you're suggesting I don't work, is that it?

I have heard with admiring submission the experience of the lady who declared that the sense of being perfectly well dressed gives a feeling of inward tranquillity which religion is powerless to bestow.

Ralph Waldo Emerson

The rush of power to the head is not as becoming as a new hat.

Helen van Slyke

That your work is somehow more important than mine, just because you get paid for it?' Quentin is full of wounded pride, incredulous at the insult.

The unfriendliness of society to his activity is difficult for the artist to accept.

Mark Rothko

'I get evaluated for my work – that's the difference. I do stuff that I don't choose to do, but that I have to do in order to earn a living. You suit yourself what you do and when you do it. That's okay by me – that's your choice. But don't come moaning to me that it doesn't pay enough or that you want my bloody taxes to prop you up in your chosen vocation. Anyway, I thought poverty was supposed to be good for artists!'

Quentin's eyes are moist, and he is breathing rapidly through his nostrils. John comes to the rescue.

'Now hang about – don't tell me you don't appreciate art, Siobhàn; that you don't read books or listen to music or go to art exhibitions? Well, then, if these people are all contributing to your enjoyment, and to the good of the community, why haven't they got a right to a decent income as well? What's happened to your precious user-pays principle now?'

'That's what royalties are for,' retorts Siobhàn. 'Anyway, Quentin here doesn't depend on income from his writing – his gran left him some money. So he's living off income earned by someone else. All income has to be *earned*, doesn't it? By someone, somewhere. That's the point.'

John looks at Quentin, who gives every appearance of being about to burst into tears. 14 Instead, he stands, walks around the table, and takes a deep breath. 'Let me tell you a story,' he says.

The notes are still there, and they still make sense. Tasha had woken at 3.00 in the morning with it staring her in the face. The code sequence that she'd been struggling with all week. Doing it wasn't the problem – it was doing it well. Making the code sexy. Getting the silicon to sing. Suddenly she was awake, and it was all there. Just a matter of getting it all down on paper. It wasn't the first time this had happened, which is why she kept a notebook beside the bed.

She reads through it again, and breaks into a broad grin. So obvious. Clear, concise, direct. There was nothing gave her quite the buzz of tight programming, after all these years. Well, almost nothing.

There's a phone jack in her room where she logs on to pick up the email. The others are always complaining about the phone being engaged. Hard lines. She scans through the stuff from the discussion groups which makes up the bulk of it. Mostly crap. But one from Tim, her brother. Enjoying life as a builder in Sydney. Ending another relationship. Still talking about coming over for Christmas.

She glances briefly at the photos on the wall, and swallows hard. Then grabs her shoulder bag with the notebook and heads towards the smell of coffee.

> **All programmers are optimists. Perhaps this modern sorcery especially attracts those who believe in happy endings and fairy godmothers.**
> Frederick P. Brooks

· · · · · · · · · ·

'I was fifteen. We all knew my gran was dying — she'd been ill for quite a while, and she'd had a good run, so no one was overly sad. It was good that she could die at home. My mother was keen for us each to say our goodbyes to her before she died, but I was scared.

'I'd never seen a dead or dying person before, and the way everyone was talking in hushed voices made it sound all the more scary. All the curtains were drawn in her room — I suppose it was because the light hurt her eyes — but it made the place seem spooky. And my gran had emphysema, which made her breathing sound like Darth Vader with bronchitis — a real death rattle. You were sure that every breath was going to be the last. There would be long pauses between her breathing, and every time you thought she was dead there'd be another gurgle and away she'd go again.

Death does not take the old but the ripe.
Russian proverb

'I loved her. I had good memories of holidays with her. My grandfather had died before I was born, so I only knew Gran. She was stern and a bit strict, but with a heart of gold. I was always on a fuss when I stayed there, with huge breakfasts in bed, you know the sort of thing. Anyway, I found it hard to make the connection between the woman I'd known and this wizened body propped up on the bed.

'My mother half-pushed me through the door to talk with her on my own. Gran was having a couple of hours of remission or something, and was reasonably cogent for a little while. So there I was, alone in the dark room with my heart pounding. I went and sat on the bed and held her hand. She opened her eyes and looked at me, and for the first time I could see that it was still *her*, you know?

'I didn't know what to say, but I still remember the hot tears and my embarrassment at them. Gran looked like she was summoning every last bit of strength and willpower in order to talk.'

Quentin pauses and takes a mouthful of coffee. Siobhàn is spellbound, her eyes shining in wonder. John is staring fixedly at the table. Claire is coiling a strand of hair around her finger.

'She told me that she'd left some money for me. Then she told me a family secret. Her first-born son had been born "out of wedlock". She was eighteen, and from a well-off family. When she got pregnant, it was a complete disaster. They sent her away to stay with her auntie. It was a difficult birth and, at the end of it all, she just had time to learn that she'd had a son before they took the baby away.

'It was the doors swinging on the hinges that she remembered, just after her boy had disappeared. No one ever talked to her about it again. It was a forbidden subject in the family. She told me that her baby had had long fingers, and that she'd always imagined him to be an artist. Gran only had the two girls after she got married.

'So, she tells me, this money I'm giving you is for my lost son. I don't want you to use it for buying things, she said. I want you to use it for dreams. Do something wonderful with it. I can still remember her pleading with her eyes. I've tried to stick to what she asked. That's why I use the money for writing.'

There is a long period of silence which follows.

'Bloody hell, it's quiet in here,' says Tasha, exploding through the door. 'Like a bleeding morgue.'

Four heads turn towards her.

'What? Have I said something wrong?'

'Buncha pansy no-hopers, the lot of them. Put them in the bloody army for a year.' Tasha wipes the marmite from the side of her face.

'I like men in uniforms,' contributes Claire.

'Save me,' John asks. 'I think I've landed at a meeting of Bigots Anonymous. Hello, my name's Sandy and I hate poor people and dagoes. Spare us, puleeze. What the hell do you know about poverty, then? When's the last time you were hungry?'

'Last Tuesday,' says Tasha. 'I stayed at work till three in the morning and forgot to eat. But I was *working*, see? You wanky social workers wouldn't know a day's work if it bit you on the bum. Spend all day skiving off having cups of tea with people, helping to convince them that they're victims. Don't give me your PC bullshit. Times have changed, Johnny boy, and we're all on our own in the jungle.'

Claire is still contemplating the military look. Quentin remains communing with his ghosts, listening to the conversation via scornful remote. Siobhàn decides to enter the fray.

'Oh come on, Tasha. It's not as simple as that. I remember when you forked out the money to pay your brother's airfare to Australia. What was that about, then?'

'That's different – that's family responsibility, isn't it? Instead of expecting the government to be our fairy bloody godmother, we look after ourselves and those we're responsible for. That's exactly my point.'

'All right,' John continues. 'Here's the question then. Who are we responsible for? Who is our family? Where are you going to put the limit?'

'Me and mine,' retorts Tasha, 'Easy.'

'Okay, then. Here's the scenario. Millé is an orphan from the Bosnian war. Found wandering outside a village. No one knows who his family is, and he's in post-traumatic shock. He gets put in an orphanage, and eventually gets adopted by British parents. The parents get killed in a car accident two weeks later. He's on his own. Whose responsibility is he?'

'Well he's not mine, that's all I know.'

'Spoken like a true humanitarian,' John mutters.

'Someone will take him in,' Siobhàn suggests.

'Will they? Millé is a kid I came across last week. We're still trying to place him. No one wants a ten-year-old kid who can't speak English. Everyone talks about community care, but the

One of the saddest things is that the only thing that a man can do for eight hours a day, day after day, is work. You can't eat eight hours a day nor drink for eight hours a day nor make love for eight hours – all you can do for eight hours is work. Which is the reason why man makes himself and everybody else so miserable and unhappy.

William Faulkner

point is there is no community anymore. Precisely because of the sort of attitude so helpfully displayed by Tasha.'

'Serbian girls are beautiful,' Claire observes. 'They have the most fantastic cheekbones.'

'Ignore her,' says Siobhàn. 'So what are you trying to say, John? That it's our problem? That we should take Millé in?'

'We can't,' laughs Tasha. 'John's just taken his room.'

'I'm saying that we have some sort of responsibility for what happens to the people around us, and that to deny it is to become less human. I'm saying that without compassion there's no such thing as society; that we become just animals in a jungle.'

'I do believe that's where I came in,' says Tasha. 'And where I'm bowing out. I have to go to work, to support a whole army of bludgers.'

Back in his room, Quentin is writing. The vaults have opened and it is flowing. His fingers race to keep up with the stream. It is unfolding before him as he writes.

He is scared to breathe unless he disturbs something. At any moment this fragile instant of creation could collapse beneath him. The words might spin sideways and back up against each other. The channel might constrict and choke. It has happened before.

For now he is catching the current. Drifting in a flood of characters and ideas and dialogue.

What value has compassion that does not take its object in its arms?

Antoine de Saint-Exupéry

Watching it emerge mysteriously on the screen before him. Where does it come from, this rush?

Claire is tapping her fingers on the steering wheel, in time to the music. She squints at the traffic lights, which remain oblivious and red. She looks out the corner of her eye at the car next to her, and is repulsed by the sight of a man picking his nose.

What was that all about, back at the flat? I haven't seen Tasha that wound up for ages. Poor Quentin. His gran sounded nice. Why hasn't he mentioned her before? This new guy has got us all stirred up. I do wish he'd do something about his hair though. It's sooo last year.

I don't know why he's going on about the homeless. It's not as if he's homeless. People get too wrapped up in ideas and things. Why can't he just enjoy himself? Probably needs... well, a bit of attention.

Oh god. We left him alone with Siobhàn.

She should be at work by now. Still, no one much cares. As long as she delivers, and she worked late a couple of nights last week. Siobhàn is awake, in every sense of the word.

John is going straight to a client's house, and doesn't need to be there till ten. He rolls a smoke, glancing up at the bleached-blonde head bobbing behind the paper.

'Mind?' he asks, nodding at the cigarette.

'Not supposed to in common areas, but I won't

I am my brother's keeper, and he's sleeping pretty rough these days.
Derek Worlock

Do not fear death so much, but rather the inadequate life.
Bertolt Brecht

tell if you don't.' She lowers the paper and smiles at him. Takes a moment to scrutinize his face. Could be all right.

'You're very committed, aren't you?' she asks through the haze.

'There's some stuff I believe in, yeah. Not so's I want everyone to think like me. But enough to stick up for a point of view. How about you?'

'Me? I'm just a graphic designer. A Dublin girl who escaped. I believe in Elvis, Bart Simpson and Coca Cola. I'm committed to virginity, as long as it doesn't affect me. I feel passionate about Guinness, but not enough to die for it.'

John is grinning, and picking up some vibes. Hormonal overdrive. It's irrepressible.

'I get the feeling you were beginning to change sides back there. Have an attack of conscience?' he wants to know.

'I'm conscience-deficient, I'm afraid. Tried to get some vitamins for it, but nothing works. Nah, I'm just a sucker for a good story, that's all. I wanted to give Quentin a cuddle. That and I like to be on the other side against Tasha. She's such a puritan.'

'Puritan? That wouldn't have been a description that leapt into my imagination.'

'She is though. Workaholic. Atoning for something, you can be sure. I like her a lot, but she's a secular Jesuit, if that means anything to you.'

'Mmm. And Quentin? Is he gay?'

'That's the question, isn't it? I would have

An isolated outbreak of virginity is a rash on the face of society. It arouses only pity from the married, and embarrassment from the single.

Charlotte Bingham

said so, except that he falls in love with women twice a week on average. They're always unattainable, and the ones that aren't he isn't interested in.' There's a flicker of something in her brown eyes. 'So it could be that he's gay and doesn't know it, or he isn't and he does, or maybe he's bi. So many possibilities these days, aren't there?'

'And you?'

'Me? I'm as hetero as a horse on heat. Been sniffing round boys since before it was decent. God, you don't beat around the bush, do you, John? Only been here five minutes and you've got us scrapping over the breakfast table and divulging our sexual histories.'

'Sorry – I'm just inquisitive, is all. Interested in things.'

'No need to apologize, at least not to me. I like a good barney – it's bred into me. I like a lot of things. This morning was good. Half the time we don't even talk to each other, but you had us firing on all cylinders. It's not a bad thing to talk about real issues now and again. I enjoy thinking about that sort of stuff.'

'What sort of stuff?'

'You know, deep stuff.'

'Ah.'

Tasha runs it again. Yes, perfect. I'm a bloody genius.

She leans back in her office chair, clasps her hands behind her head and sighs. The screen

Love is the answer, but while you're waiting for the answer, sex raises some pretty good questions.

Woody Allen

dissolves into fractal patterns. There is a deep satisfaction in solving problems.

Below the surface there is something niggling. She prods it out of hiding. That damned wanky lefty smartass. Full of righteous bullshit. He's got under my skin.

The memory comes unsummoned, unwelcome. Not far from the entrance to work. A man sitting on a blanket with a small cardboard sign next to him. A plate with a few coins. And she could smell his sweet sherry breath, even while trying to ignore him. It made her furious. She wanted to kick him.

There are other thoughts, other memories swirling in the undercurrent.

Tasha closes her eyes before snapping them wide open. It usually works. She makes her way to the coffee machine and dials up espresso.

John pauses for a minute as he closes the front door behind him. Turns and looks back at the house before venturing into the street.

Yes. I think I'm going to enjoy my time here.

Chapter Two

'Friday night,' Quentin suggests.

'Who's going to cook?' Tasha wants to know. Not that there's much danger of anyone asking her to take it on.

'*Moi*, natch,' declares Quentin. 'Siobhàn and the new boy are on for it. Claire thinks it will *destroy* her social life, but she'll do it *just for me*.'

'You do have a way with women, Quent baby. Okay, count me in.'

'Supremo. It's a done deal.'

The oil is extra virgin. God knows what that involves. Cool and green and clear. Quentin drizzles it into the bowl from a great height. He grinds fresh black pepper into it.

He slices capsicum with pleasure. Enjoys the crisp cutting of the knife. Cooking. It's better than foreplay.

There are small bowls of ingredients scattered across the bench. A glorious mix of colours and textures and smells. Ah, the anticipation.

Some are too large and obtrusive. Others minimalist to the point of non-existence. You can end up with a come-on or a turn-off.

Alone in the lounge, with only the all-seeing eye for company, Claire practises her wave.

She is a student of the wave. The small gesture

Quentin's Salad Dressing

Half a cup of olive oil (degree of virginity according to personal taste)

A dash of white vinegar (tartish, not virginal in the least)

One teaspoon dried tarragon

Half teaspoon salt

Freshly ground black pepper

2 cloves garlic, crushed

Combine ingredients. Mix thoroughly. Apply to salad at the very last moment.

of the hand to acknowledge one's fame. From wrist-twisting to the grand circle, Claire has observed and explored them all. It's what she looks for at premières and fame-fests.

Personally, she likes the understated approach. The 'Oh god it's so boring, but I must acknowledge the peasants who adore me,' complete with Mona Lisa smile/grimace. She tries it once again.

One day, it may be necessary. Who can tell?

John pokes his head into the kitchen, inhaling the promise.

'Need a hand with anything?'

Quentin swivels on one heel, with an outstretched arm bearing a kitchen knife. It points somewhere in the region of John's navel.

'Out! Out of my kitchen, you hear?'

John tugs his forelock and retreats.

'All right, Rupert. Let's break it down. What part of "I'm busy tonight" don't you understand?'

Siobhàn walks as she talks, stepping out the points as they are made. The portable telephone was invented for her.

'Look, I might have said a lot of things, you know? *Post coitum, omni crapola.*'

'Never mind. Please don't make this hard for me. I like you a lot; you're a nice boy as far as boys go. But you may have put more on this than I did. I'm a bit of a free spirit, you know? I like to keep my options open.'

26

'No, I don't think sex necessarily implies a relationship. Do you? Honestly?'

'Well, I'm sorry, Rupert. I don't want to be a bitch. Oh shit. Please don't cry.'

He can hear the voices from the lounge, where he's organized nibbles and drinks. Everything is in order.

A last taste of the sauce. Superb. As it should be.

Let the evening begin.

'This stuff is crap. Who bought it?' Tasha demands.

'I confess. It was cheap at the supermarket,' John explains.

'At the supermarket? You don't buy wine at the bloody supermarket, you big prat. Someone crack a new bottle before we all die from anti-freeze.'

'Serve you right, neglecting mother's nectar,' suggests Siobhàn, wiping the Guinness froth from her mouth with the back of a hand.

'I wish I could afford to be sophisticated,' says John.

The pot plant is doing much better, he notes while opening the bottle. Amazing what a little care will do.

Tasha drains her glass and waves it menacingly at John. Claire is draped artfully across a chair, in her usual reverie. Quentin appears at the door, beaming.

'Well, children, we can eat soon. But first the rules.'

> **Life is rather like a tin of sardines – we're all of us looking for the key.**
>
> Alan Bennett

'Rules?' splutters Siobhàn, choking on a mouthful of cracker and pâté. 'What is this, a bondage game?'

'You should be so lucky,' continues Quentin, unfazed. 'I organized the dinner, I'm the cook, and so tonight I make the rules. Now I'm sick of chitty chatty bullshit; besides which I need some inspiration for my writing. So. This is going to be a serious dinner, and we're going to have some serious discussion.'

'*Sieg Heil*', contributes Siobhàn.

'What do you mean?' asks Claire, immediately regretting her choice of perfume.

'I mean, darling, that we are going to have a discussion of some substance while we eat. We shall feed ourselves on every level. Well, perhaps not *every* level, but at least a few. And tonight's issue, should you choose to accept it, is money.'

'Ah, the root of all evil,' warns Tasha.

'Not accurate,' says John. 'The phrase you're thinking of is "The *love of money* is the root of all evil."'

'Well, excuse me. Some of us are not so well versed in scripture as your Royal Highness.'

'What is this?' groans Claire. 'I mean, have we agreed to it already? Only I was expecting to have a nice dinner, not to talk about politics or whatever…'

'We haven't quite got that far yet, but no doubt it will come,' Quentin predicts. 'What do the rest of you think?'

'I'm in,' says John.

Siobhàn raises a thumb. Tasha nods. Four pairs of eyes turn on Claire, who crumples in annoyed resignation. Quentin sits on the floor next to her.

'We made a bit of a start the other morning. And it got me thinking. Money seems to be centre-stage in life. It's all over the news. All our heroes are rich people. Most of us spend our lives trying to get more of it. But nobody much talks about it. So here we are – a golden opportunity.'

'What's there to talk about?' asks Tasha. 'It's lovely stuff. Makes the world go round. I plan to earn bucketloads of dosh, and stash away everything I don't spend. Money buys freedom and power, and shopping's better than sex.'

'That's it?' John wants to know. 'That's your philosophy of life? You make Imelda Marcos sound like a humanitarian. You talk like selfishness was a virtue.'

'Here we go again,' says Siobhàn.

Quentin is grinning.

I think whoever said money can't buy happiness simply hadn't found out where to go shopping.

Bo Derek

They arrive to find the table set. A plain metal candleholder with two candles is in the centre. Quentin lights the candles amidst the banter and scraping of chairs. Two bottles of red wine are open on the table, as well as one of sauvignon blanc. A glass jug with iced and limed water sits beaded with condensation.

'All right – ceasefire while I run through the menu for tonight. We start with filo parcels of herbed chicken, accompanied by a blue cheese sauce. Then we will move on to saddle of lamb with rosemary, pepper and parmesan. The sauce is plum-based with a few special extras. We have for you oven-baked potatoes with a mushroom filling, and a dressed salad of fresh greens. Dessert will be introduced when it arrives. Enjoy.'

The chorus of approval gradually subsides as the wine is poured and the food delivered. It swells again as first mouthfuls are savoured and acclaimed.

The candlelight makes the glasses sparkle and the wine glow in ruby satisfaction. Harsh sounds of implements striking crockery are masked by the more festive murmur of conversation. Eyes brighten as a slow transformation begins. A meal is happening.

'My old man was on the dole for ten years when I was young,' explains Siobhàn. 'We had nothing. Mum used to water the milk down – true. Made it go twice as far. She used to do housework for a woman up the road to earn a few extra quid, so's she could buy school stuff for all us kids. Dad always seemed to have enough for the pub. It wasn't till I was about thirteen that I suddenly realized we were poor. I'd just thought that everyone lived like that. I don't think it made much difference to us in the end. We all had a good time anyway.'

'Yeah, it's a fact that a lot of people with no money still enjoy life,' says John. 'Some of the people I work with have a joy in life that puts me to shame. And the parties are to die for. It's complete crap that you need money to be happy.'

Tasha hones in like a mosquito on a sniff of blood.

'Oh, here we go with the noble poor. You can't be serious. The only people who are happy in poverty are those with no imagination. Money's about choice. You give anyone the choice between porridge and eggs benedict for breakfast, or a decent car over the bus, or a room each for their kids instead of having them all in together, and you know which way they're going to choose. This idea that the rich must all be bored and unhappy is working-class fantasy. It's a way of living in misery without topping yourself.'

'My parents were well-off, I suppose you'd have to say,' Claire contributes for the first time. 'I don't think I'd describe them as happy.'

'Some rich people lack imagination as much as poor people,' Tasha admits.

'Aha,' John crows. 'So it's not the money which decides happiness, then.'

'Is there any more of that sauce?' Siobhàn wants to know. 'I don't want to lick my plate, but I will if I have to.'

'Did anyone see *The Magic Christian*?' asks Quentin, slicing the meat.

'Yes, yes, yes,' says Siobhàn, bouncing on her seat. 'Peter Sellers and Ringo Starr. A classic.'

'Was it a film?' Claire inquires.

'It's about a squillionaire,' Siobhàn continues, 'who decides to get the help of a bum to give away all his money. There's this great scene, where they go

I'd like to live like a poor man, but with a lot of money.
Pablo Picasso

into an art shop with wanky assistants doing their limp-wristed thing. The two big spenders take a shine to the most expensive painting in the shop, a portrait, and decide to buy it. The manager is falling over himself with joy, and wants to know if it should be packed. But they say no, and pull out a pocket knife. And then they just cut the nose out of the canvas. "I only liked the nose," says one of them.'

'How about the last bit?' Quentin prompts, delivering another perfectly pink slice onto a white plate.

Money doesn't talk, it swears.
Bob Dylan

'They set up this huge tank,' Siobhàn obliges, 'a big round swimming-pool sort of thing. And then they fill it with all the most disgusting stuff – raw sewage, blood and effluent from the abattoir, that sort of thing. When it's good and full, they dump thousands and thousands of pounds into the centre of it, and stand back to watch the fun. People are climbing over each other and wading through all this shit just to get at the money.'

'Siobhàn, that's gross,' complains Claire.

'It was bloody hilarious,' says Quentin.

'The point being?' Tasha wants to know.

'That we're totally obsessed with money,' explains Siobhàn, 'and that we'll crawl through slime to get at it.'

'Filthy lucre,' giggles Quentin, 'in every sense of the word.'

'My own philosophy, such as it is,' offers John, 'is that one should wipe one's arse with a fifty-pound note every year. Helps to put everything in perspective.'

'Bullshit. I bet you don't,' Tasha challenges.

'Try me,' John answers.

'Guys, please can we clean this up?' Claire wails. 'Quentin's gone to all the trouble to cook us this beautiful meal, and all we can talk about...'

'Don't worry, Claire, I'm not going to make him wipe his bum at the table. But I bet he wouldn't burn fifty quid.'

Tasha fixes him with her eye and smirks. She's beginning to enjoy this conversation.

'I would, but I haven't got a fifty,' says John lamely.

'You give it back to me in whatever notes you've got, and I'll get you a fifty-quid note from my room,' Tasha is keen to suggest.

'You're on.'

'It's the Queen I was thinking of,' mutters Claire.

There's a hushed silence as they linger over the final mouthfuls of lamb. Attention keeps drifting to the single note of currency which Tasha has propped up against the candleholder.

'It's only money,' says John, taking a generous slug of wine.

He grips the note by one corner, and holds it high above the candles. The silence deepens, and gathers portent. John stares hard at Tasha as he lowers his hand.

'Golly,' says Claire, quickly covering her mouth in embarrassment.

The corner takes a surprisingly long time to

> It's fine to make money. It isn't fine to make money your God.
> Sinead O'Connor

> It's important to me that money not be important to me.
> Les Brown

catch. Eventually a blue and green flame begins to lick up the surface. Before it burns his hand, John lowers it onto an empty plate. He is surprised to see what look like tears welling in Tasha's eyes. They all stare, unable to look away, as the money shrivels into blackness. The printed details still show on the remains.

'Burns just like any other paper,' says John.

'That was weird,' suggests Quentin.

'Almost sacrilegious,' agrees Siobhàn.

John grins slowly as he stirs the ashes with a fork. It comes, it goes, it is gone.

'My point, exactly,' he says. 'It's a good way to get in touch with how you feel about money.'

'I just hope you've still got the bloody rent money,' Tasha says sharply.

There is definitely evidence of tears, despite her backhanded attempt to remove it.

'Anyone for more wine?' asks Quentin.

'I used to go into her purse on benefit day. She'd always get drunk, and then in the morning she had no idea of how much she'd spent the day before. I'd stash it away and use it later in the week to buy food when the money was all gone. Otherwise the boys would have starved. I could never tell whether she knew what I was doing or not.'

Tasha pauses to dab her eyes where something has leaked out. She uses a paper serviette.

'One night she came into my room while I was

34

counting it. I must have had about ten quid or something. She hit the bloody roof. Called me a thieving little bitch, told me I was just like my father, and started knocking me around. I wouldn't let go of the money, and we had a tug of war over it. I can still remember her face so close to mine – the look in her eyes and the smell of her breath. She won, of course, and then she took me into the kitchen and made me watch while she burned the money on the fire. Said it would be my fault if we went hungry.'

John has gone very quiet.

'It wasn't till I was older that I found out what an alcoholic was. I just thought she was a drunk. I still do, in a way. Too many excuses made for people.'

Siobhàn has reached out a hand to hold Tasha's. Quentin is behind her massaging her neck.

'That's enough maudlin exposé from me. But money was what we needed, you see? We didn't have enough for living. So I can never think of it with detachment.'

'I like to buy things,' declares Claire.

'We've noticed, darling,' says Quentin without sarcasm.

'No, I mean I really enjoy it. I think most people do, don't they? Getting something new, taking it home all wrapped up, and then opening it up and enjoying the fact that you now own it. It cheers you up, doesn't it? I've known women come into the shop looking grey and haggard, and

I have enough money to last me the rest of my life. Unless I buy something.

Cher

half an hour later they leave with a new outfit, absolutely radiant.'

John blinks at her, twice.

'So your dress shop is actually providing a public service?'

'In a manner of speaking, yes.' She pouts at him, well aware of the irony. 'I don't see what's wrong with making people happy.'

'The problem is, you see,' John expounds, 'that if money or shopping is what it takes to make people happy, then only certain people will be happy, because only certain people have money. That seems just a little unfair to me.'

'But that's not my problem, is it? I'm not responsible for who's got money and who hasn't. Not everyone wants to change the world, John. I'm content to brighten up my little corner of it if I can.'

'Claire, listen to yourself. You're opting out. Shopping is a distraction, don't you see? It's escapism, like taking drugs or bonking out of boredom. You're just trying to grab something to cheer yourself up so you won't have to face a world you don't like.'

'So? I don't like the world the way it is — why should I? It's horrible.'

'Well do something about it! Change it! Don't run away into a corner and hide.'

'I am doing something — I'm trying to make it more beautiful. That's what I do.'

'You can't make a corpse beautiful with cosmetics.'

'Yes, you can. And what's that supposed to mean, anyway?'

'Are you sure you're not religious, John?' Quentin breaks in.

John picks up the wine glass and swirls it in front of him. He watches the slow creep of alcohol up the side of the glass. The candlelight is refracted into red patterns drifting across his face.

'Who said I wasn't religious?' he counters.

'You don't sound very religious,' Siobhàn says, squinting at him.

'I'm a bit religious,' tenders Claire.

'You're right, I'm not religious at all,' John decides. 'I'm no different from any of you. Anyway, we're getting off the subject. Can't you see that being good little consumers is the modern equivalent of slavery? Every time you go and buy something for therapy you're putting another link in the chain.'

'That's a bit rich, isn't it?' objects Siobhàn. 'I don't quite see how my picking up a new CD is on the same level as people being shipped halfway across the world and abused for the rest of their lives.'

'Depends a bit who you listen to,' offers Quentin.

'Look, who runs this world?' John asks. 'Do you think it's governments? It's not even the military any more. It's Nike and Coca-Cola and Microsoft. The whole bloody world is in economic slavery. What do you think brought communism down? Democracy? No, it was Levi jeans. Why have we

We must respect the other fellow's religion, but only in the same sense and to the extent that we respect his theory that his wife is beautiful and his children smart.

H.L. Mencken

all gone for New Right economics? Who wins and who loses? Who gets the benefits of free trade? Why are all the democratic powers electing rulers who look good and have no political philosophy? Ask yourself. Don't just sit around being depressed and buying stuff!'

'Here endeth the lesson,' quips Siobhàn.

'I still don't see what's wrong with working in a dress shop,' says Claire.

Siobhàn has been watching John as he speaks. The fire in his eyes, the colour in his cheeks. The way he leans forward. The intensity in his voice. Passion.

It makes her pleasantly warm around the throat area. Another sip of wine, and she licks her lips, slowly.

'So,' says Quentin, 'back to me. I think you're sounding just a *touch* paranoid, John. A little bit of conspiracy theory, *n'est-ce pas*? Personally, I don't feel manipulated at all. Not by the multinationals, anyway. Most of us know what's going on, and we pretend to play along for our own benefit. We look like good consumers, but underneath it all we don't give a shit. The world's poked, all right; that's a given. But we're going to go down in style, raiding the little fashion houses as we go. Okay, from the outside it looks as if we've bought the whole deal, but in fact we've bought none of it. We're just organizing a dance party on the Titanic.'

'Yeah, that sounds good,' agrees Siobhàn, 'I'll go with that.'

Tasha is still staring somewhat blankly. Rummaging around in old closets leaves a lot to be cleaned up. She can hear the conversation as if it is on TV.

Claire has lost the thread of the discussion once more. She watches the way Quentin runs a finger across the top of his glass, and wonders again.

'But what's the difference?' John demands. 'What difference is there between you agreeing with the system or not? Buying the stuff is what keeps the system alive. You think McDonalds gives a shit whether you believe in their corporate philosophy? Of course not. They're just counting how many burgers you well-heeled rebels throw down your throats. They'll even make a rebel-burger if they think it'll sell. Enclose a free figurine of Fidel Castro.'

'So you don't eat McDonalds, then?' Quentin asks almost innocently.

'Screw you,' retorts John, drawing a raised eyebrow from Quentin. 'That's not the point, is it? The point is that I feel *guilty* when I eat it, not like I'm somehow saving the world.'

'You *are* religious,' Siobhàn decides.

'Time,' opines Quentin, 'for dessert.'

He opens the refrigerator and begins delivering parfait glasses around the table.

'What we have here is two varieties of melon,

McDonald's is good for the world, that's my opinion.

Oliver Stone

Quentin's Mango Cream

One can mango slices, drained

One cup of natural yoghurt

One tablespoon honey

Half cup fresh cream

Blend ingredients together. Chill before serving (the sauce and its maker).

accompanied by a home-made coconut vanilla ice-cream, and gloriously topped with my special mango cream.'

Claire ends her internal debate by deciding not to refuse. It's fruit, after all. How bad can that be?

Siobhàn drops her spoon and stoops to retrieve it. On the way back to the surface her head somehow makes contact with John's lap.

'Sorry,' she says, holding his eye for a second longer than is necessary, and smiling.

'And,' Quentin remembers, 'a little bit of dessert wine to go with it.'

Tasha is back in the fray. Her previous glass of wine has not lasted as long as it might.

'Here's the way I see it. Before money there was trade, right? People would swap something they owned or had made for whatever someone else had that they wanted. Then it got a bit complicated, as it does, 'cos A had x to trade, which B wanted, but A wanted y, which C had lots of.'

'You what?' complains Siobhàn.

'No, listen. So money's a way of making the trading circle bigger. It *represents* something. Using money, B can buy y off C and sell it to A, and then buy x.'

'Where did eggs come into it?' Claire wants to know.

Money, it turned out, was exactly like sex, you thought of nothing else if you didn't have it, and thought of other things if you did.

James Baldwin

'Shaddup. Money stands for the work or talent or whatever. It's a symbol, that's all. I work with symbols all the time. They're useful, as long as you don't take them too seriously and always remember they stand for something else.'

'Okay, okay, okay,' John chants. 'That's maybe how money started out. But what does it stand for now? An American currency player buys and sells money eight times in twenty-four hours and makes a million dollars. What does that million dollars represent, then? His work? Hardly. His knowledge? Maybe, but is it worth the combined lifetime earnings of a hundred Somalians? And what are we talking about when we get into buying money? Do we need a new symbol?'

'Nah, we've already got one,' Tasha concedes. 'It's called power. That's the universal symbol.'

'Preee-cisely. I don't believe this; we agree on something.'

'Yeah well, don't get too cocky, John-boy. I haven't become a bleeding-heart liberal yet. What's wrong with power?'

'Nothing at all, as long as it's spread around. It's like horseshit, Tasha. Spread it round and it helps things grow; stack it up in one place and it stinks.'

'Bullshit, more like. How do you think evolution happens, then, eh? You think they take a vote on it in committee? We'd all still be sliding around the pond chanting about amoebic rights.'

'This is heavenly,' says Claire. 'The dessert, I mean,' she adds in the sudden quiet.

'I have,' Quentin announces, 'the acid question. Fanfare please.'

> The meek shall inherit the earth, but not the mineral rights.
>
> John Paul Getty

Cutlery dances to the rhythm of hands beating
on the table.

'And the question is – for two million pounds,
a holiday in Jamaica and an evening with Margaret
Thatcher – fingers on the buzzers please – wait
for it – is there anything money can't buy?'

'Too easy,' chimes in Siobhàn. 'Money can't buy
me love.'

'But it will get you phone sex,' Tasha counters.

'Doesn't count,' says Siobhàn. 'We're talking
love, not lust.'

'Hmm... I'm not even convinced on the love
front,' Quentin ponders. 'Let's take a woman,
maybe fifty years old. Her husband dies, she's
filthy rich and she gets lonely. So she advertises
for a companion – a younger man. The guys who
respond are only in it for one thing – the money.
She picks one out. The deal is that he has to live
with her, and in turn she pays for all his expenses
– travel, food, clothes, the lot. When he takes it
on he figures he's just got to grit his teeth for the
sake of the dosh. If he gets bored he can always
shoot through. But being around with her all the
time, he finds out what a wonderful, interesting
generous person she is. He hears some of her
stories, and gets to tell his own to someone who
listens. The lovemaking is a damn sight better
than he ever hoped for. Gradually he stops seeing
her as an older woman, as his employer, as a ticket
to wealth. And he realizes he's fallen in love with
her. She, of course, is well satisfied. She has what
she wanted – love. Without the money he

wouldn't have come. So there it is — she's purchased love.'

'But hang on,' Siobhàn objects, 'it might have turned out differently, mightn't it? The guy could have been a real arsehole — treated her like crap, used her money and taken off for the hills. There's no guarantee, is there? Doesn't matter how much money she's got, she can't make anyone love her.'

'Siobhàn's right,' says John. She smiles and leans into his shoulder. 'There's a lot of stuff money can't buy. Love, contentment, trust, hope... They're not commodities, thank God. The sickness of our world is in trying to make them into something that can be sold.'

'Maybe you can't buy them,' Tasha says with an edge to her voice, 'but money goes a long way towards covering up their absence.'

'Does it?' asks Quentin.

'Yes, it damn well does.' She is adamant.

In the silence, Claire speaks.

'My father was away a lot. On business trips, you know. Mummy was neurotic, I suppose you'd say — she was tense all the time. Every now and again she would explode in anger, and you were never quite sure what it would take to set her off. I was always pleased to see Daddy come home, because he was calm and gentle. He would bring me a present when he came back. I always remember it the same way — he would come in the front door, and I would go running to meet him. Just as I got to him, he would pull out some present from behind his back and put it in my

> **The only thing money gives you is the freedom of not worrying about money.**
> Johnny Carson

> **Money is better than poverty, if only for financial reasons.**
> Woody Allen

arms. I would pretend to be happy, and I suppose I was. But what I really wanted — I've never said this before — what I really wanted was a cuddle. My parents never touched much. I had everything I wanted — dolls, bikes, clothes — but never cuddles.'

'At least you had a father,' says Tasha quietly.

'I'm sorry,' says Claire.

'Oh God,' says John.

Siobhàn slides her hand into John's, out of sight. Claire places her arm around Tasha, who is taking a close interest in her empty glass. Quentin draws patterns on the table, wondering how to get back from here.

'Well let's not get bloody morbid about it,' Tasha suggests at last. 'How about some of that Kirsch, Quentin? I'm all for escapism.'

'I'll drink to that,' says John.

'Ah, so you're caving in to the force of my superior reason,' gloats Tasha.

'I'm laying down my weapons for the sake of friendship.'

'You may need to raise them again shortly for the sake of love,' Tasha chuckles, looking accusingly at Siobhàn.

'Tasha!' Claire rebukes, alert to the overtones.

'I'm a witness that no money has changed hands. Who's for coffee?' Quentin asks.

'It's been good,' Tasha concedes.

'Thanks for the meal, Quentin, it was wonderful. You're a brilliant cook,' smiles Claire.

If all the economists were laid end to end they still wouldn't reach a conclusion.

George Bernard Shaw

'I've enjoyed it,' he responds. 'Thanks for going along with it all. I don't know that we've sorted much out, but the blag was certainly entertaining.'

'We can't just leave it there,' complains Siobhàn. We have to do it again.'

'I was hoping someone might want to,' says Quentin. 'It just so happens that I have a plan. What say we do this every Friday night for a while? Different person cook each time, and the cook chooses the topic of discussion. What do you reckon?'

'Do I have to cook?' whines Tasha.

'Does it have to be Fridays?' joins in Claire.

'Absolutely,' decides Siobhàn. 'I bags next week.'

'You people are great,' says John. 'I'm sorry if I mouth off so much. It's just the way I find out what I believe.'

'It's okay, John,' Siobhàn responds. 'We won't throw you out just yet.'

> People find life entirely too time-consuming.
> Stanislaw J. Lec

Chapter Three

John wakes naked and hot. A digital red display informs him that it's 3.17 a.m. He's sweating. Intense sexual activity seems to disturb whatever temperature monitoring system his body is operating on. That, and the fact that Siobhàn is backed up into him and purring. His head is thick with wine and sex.

He turns onto his back, staring into the blackness. Something within is screaming for nicotine. His post-coital ease is disturbed by deeper troubles. Thoughts unwind from the centre and begin to crawl across his mind.

How do these things happen? You bump up against someone — hardly have time to find out who they are — and then you wake up in bed next to them. Neither of you have touched your loneliness. The sex has been good — wild, ecstatic. But it's like you're trying to screw the sorrow out of your gut, and you never quite get there. What's gone wrong with intimacy when it still leaves you feeling alone?

Belinda's face looms in his imagination. He feels his chest constrict. The present disappears down the throat of memory. Longing. And nothing to satisfy it.

Siobhàn turns towards him, and drapes a leg across him. He kisses the side of her head. Forgive me, he mouths to himself, and anyone else who cares to hear.

The body is a house of many windows: there we all sit, showing ourselves and crying on the passers-by to come and love us.

Robert Louis Stevenson

·········

She notices the door to John's room is ajar, and pokes her head around it. The bed is unslept in. It's so predictable. But why then, Tasha interrogates herself, does it make you so bloody angry?

There's the makings of a story emerging from the psychic sludge. Quentin wakes to feel its skeleton. He has learned to salvage this early-morning flotsam. There is a notebook and pen beside the bed.

A man gets out of prison. He's learned two things while inside. The first is the rudimentary art of tattooing. The second is how to condense his feelings into poetry. His poems are very good, but he can't make a living out of them. So he sets up shop as a tattooist, and earns enough to get by on. But all the time his mind is preoccupied with the making of poems.

It so happens that a woman comes in, and wants a tattoo of a seagull on her thigh. They get to talking, go out for a drink, and eventually she ends up moving in with him. He wakes up one morning with the first line of a poem, and an image of what he must do with it. No matter how hard he works on it, he can't get further than the first line.

After a while he talks to his partner about the crazy idea that has come to him. She agrees, and so he tattoos the first line of his poem onto her

True poetry, the best of it, is but the ashes of a burnt-out passion.

Oliver Wendell Holmes

The poem is the dream made flesh.

Henry Miller

back. A week later, the second line has come, and he adds it to the first. It's his best work ever, but nothing more comes for another month. Then, after a night of passionate lovemaking, he wakes with the next line, and is able to inscribe it onto the woman's back.

This goes on for some period of time, until the poem is near completion. There's just the last line to add; which is just as well, because he's running out of room on his lover's back. The final line refuses to emerge. They decide to try and nudge it along with a night of alcohol, drugs and heavy sex.

But the woman dies in the night, of heart failure. He discovers later that there was a heart problem all along which she was aware of. The man weeps, half for his lost love, and half for the poem which can never be completed. She is buried, and he keeps no copy of what has been written on her body.

After the funeral, he comes home and tattoos on his own arm: 'It is finished.'

Quentin closes the notebook and smiles. This is a good start to the day.

At Pink Angel prices are very discreetly displayed. People who need to know the cost are probably not in the right shop. And, Claire likes to think, it keeps the emphasis on the clothes and how they look. Price is entirely secondary to style.

But today, as she prints out a sales docket for a regular customer, the total amount catches her

attention. She pauses just a moment before

tearing the slip off the machine, and considers. It makes her cross, the whole conversation about money. As if it makes any difference anyway.

'It doesn't mean anything, you know.' Siobhàn does her best to glower at John across her espresso.

'No. Fine.' John draws lines across the top of his latte with a teaspoon.

'What? Don't give me that old crap.'

'Excuse me? I was agreeing with you.'

'No you weren't. I'm Irish, I warn you. I can read sulking men at a hundred paces. So don't give me that "woe is me – she doesn't love me" stuff. We had a good night, I like you a lot, and now we've got to carry on living together in the same flat. Maybe we can do it again sometime.'

John begins to say something and then stops himself. Instead he raises his eyes and looks directly at Siobhàn. He smiles at her.

'When I was younger, I used to play rugby,' he says. 'It was a whole culture, you know, a way of life. Two games a week, two nights of practice, and a fair bit of personal training. Every Saturday night getting rolling drunk with someone vomiting out the window of the car. Usually a fistfight or two, and countless trips to the Accident & Emergency service. Lots of bravado. The guys would talk about "bunting sheilas". Most of it was wishful thinking – in the presence of women they were awkward and embarrassed. If they ever did get close to a girl, they reverted to a sort of primitive animal lust. Just needed to get

> Lust is the craving for salt of a man who is dying of thirst.
> Frederick Buechner

their rocks off and then reach for another beer. I tried to be like them, just to be part of the gang. But I never could. I hated to see people being treated like that. I'd often end up holding on to some girl who was crying her eyes out after what amounted to sexual assault by one of these rugger buggers, and maybe drive her home. I think I was considered a bit of a pansy.'

'And the point of this story is... ?'

'I'm grown up, Siobhàn. I know all about the difference between sex, relationship and commitment. So I'm not going to hang a whole heap of guilt or expectation on you. We can put last night down to harmless fun if you like. I won't remind you of it again. But I struggle with it, to be completely honest. Struggle with myself for getting into things where we're basically using each other. And I don't want either of us being on tap for a quick screw when there's nothing on TV.'

'You sneaky bastard,' retorts Siobhàn. 'Now you've got me feeling guilty. How the hell do you do that?'

She takes a pull on the coffee and sighs deeply.

'I'm sorry, John. My life's a bloody mess when it comes to men. I like men, God help me, and I like sex. I keep waking up with people I don't know — not you — I know you quite well in comparison. And I vow it won't happen again, and a couple of days later it does. And then I've got all this shit to deal with from men who want to take me to meet their mother, and send me flowers at work. I'm screwed in every sense of the word.'

She signs the card 'Your daughter, Tasha'. A little perfunctory and remote, but it's honest. She can't bring herself to use the word 'love' in relation to her mother. The weekly card is in itself a sign of something – not love perhaps, but at least duty or obligation.

Tasha is pleased that the boarding house is in another city. That way she doesn't have to make excuses for not visiting. The money, of course, is exchanged for cheap alcohol. Tasha is beyond feeling moralistic. It is the way things are. Life can't be changed, but if you use your head, it can be managed.

Cooking is not her foremost talent, but she can produce a reasonable dinner on a basic level. She toyed with the idea of doing something traditionally Irish, but dismissed that as simply too twee. So fondue it is. It usually worked, except for the time all the ingredients separated out, and she was left with clots of rubbery cheese floating on a lake of wine.

She slices the bread into cubic chunks, trying to estimate how much is needed. Probably too much, but that's the way she's been raised.

The table is arranged functionally under Siobhàn's eye. Two big slabs of breadboard on either side of the fondue burner. At either end of the table there's a fat squat beeswax candle. And,

Sian's Fondue

Rub fondue dish with half a clove of garlic.

Chop the garlic finely and place in the dish.

Add half a glass of dry white wine per person.

Add 120 grams grated cheese per person. Use two types of cheese – Emmental and Gruyère.

Stir constantly over a gentle heat until everything is melted.

Add pepper and nutmeg to taste.

Add a teaspoon of cornflour mixed in a little cold water to bind.

Serve with chunks of coarse bread.

Be careful who you sit next to.

51

naturally, Sinead O'Connor laying down the
atmosphere.

Quentin and Tasha are fencing with the fondue
forks. Tasha parries and then strikes past
Quentin's defences.

'*Voilà*,' she cries.

'I think *touché* is the word you're looking for,'
Quentin suggests.

'Whatever. You're dead meat anyway, my literary
friend. Look on the bright side: should be good
for sales.'

John has placed himself carefully between
Claire and Quentin, to avoid any embarrassing
repetitions of the previous meal's conclusion. No
one at the table is unaware of the newly
complicated *frisson*. The signals have been noted
and absorbed, though Claire remains unconvinced
that consummation has already taken place.

Siobhàn carries the steaming pot of fondue to
the table and settles it lovingly in the middle.

'Well, my loyal subjects,' she announces, 'here
are the laws of the land. You only dip your bread
in the bowl with your fork, and we're playing by
Swiss rules. That means if you drop your bread in
the mix, your penalty is that you have to kiss the
person on your right. No changing seats' –
Siobhàn pauses to look directly at John who is
eyeing Quentin – 'and deliberate dropping of
bread is not counted. And for your entertainment
and delight, the topic of conversation for
tonight's meal is, wait for it, sex.'

52

'Oh, please not,' complains Claire.

'What's to talk about?' asks Tasha. 'I thought sex became extinct in the seventies.'

'No, that was charity,' contributes John.

'Well,' declares Quentin, 'I'm in favour of it, all things considered.'

'Of what?' Claire asks.

'Sex. In general. Or anywhere else for that matter.'

'I think there's too much talk about it already,' Claire counters. 'Anyone would think that sex had just been invented, the way everyone goes on about it.'

'In a sense it has,' John joins in. 'It's only since we've had reliable contraception that people have been able to think about sex in isolation from childbearing.'

'When you say people, I expect you mean women,' Tasha interjects. 'I don't think men have ever thought about childbearing. In fact, when it comes to sex, men don't think at all. As thick as their dicks, to coin a phrase.'

'I knew this would turn out to be vulgar,' frowns Claire.

'Look, what's vulgar about it?' Siobhàn wants to know. 'Dick, fanny, tush, cock — they're all just names for bits of our bodies. It's not vulgar to talk about arms or ears or thumbs, is it? People not talking about sex is what jams up our therapy clinics. We need to get it out in the open.'

'Not at the table, puleeze,' pleads Quentin. 'You'll quite put me off my food.'

When authorities warn you of the sinfulness of sex, there is an important lesson to be learned. Do not have sex with the authorities.

Matt Groening

In the interim he makes a show of doing something to his food with his mouth in a highly suggestive manner.

'I think,' asserts Siobhàn, swallowing a mouthful of wine, 'that sex is bloody good fun, and we should all be at it whenever the opportunity arises. We're all too repressed and anal, if you'll excuse the expression. We make too much of the whole deal. Animals have got it more together than us – they just shag and then it's over. No interpretation, no expectation.'

'No magic or mystery, either,' John challenges. 'For animals it's at the level of survival. It's just an instinctive thing for the continuation of the species. I'd like to think there's a bit more to it than that.'

'I'm with John on this one,' says Tasha. 'If you reduce sex to the animal level, you reduce us to animals.'

'Or raise us to the level of animals,' counters Siobhàn.

'You're screwed whichever way you turn,' offers Quentin.

John intervenes to halt the slide of the discussion, partially out of consideration for Claire.

'Here's the scene,' he says. 'Science advances to the stage of being able to tap into the brain's communication centre. It's like virtual reality, except that it's impossible to tell the difference from reality. By hotwiring the receptors in your brain, you actually experience whatever is fed in. The possibilities are endless. But the one that occurs first is that of remote-control sex. Simply by plugging in to a headset and running the right software, you can have any partner, any experience you want. No conversational games to steer your way through, no risk of disease, no one to eat breakfast with the next day. And best of all, no failures. One hundred per cent guaranteed high-voltage orgasm every time, enough to blow your brains. As often and as long as you want it. No need to deal with a partner ever again.

'The question is this: would it be enough to make you give up on sex with real people?'

'The big O, every time? No fluids to clean up afterwards?' inquires Tasha.

'Reliable, intense, persistent and very clean,' he assures her.

'I think you just sold me one.'

'What about you, Siobhàn?' John wants to know.

'I'm not fucking a machine,' she growls.

'Very delicately put. But what, pray, is it that you get in the real thing that you wouldn't get from my so-called machine?'

'A smoke in bed afterwards.'

'I'm sure we can arrange to have that programmed in. But I suspect you mean a little more than the actual cigarette?'

'Yeah, well, it's being there with someone, isn't it? The conversation and so on. You can't make a sodding computer into a person, can you?'

··········

> **The orgasm has replaced the Cross as the focus of longing and fulfillment.**
> Malcolm Muggeridge

> **Remember, if you smoke after sex, you're doing it too fast.**
> Anonymous

'I think,' says Claire tentatively, 'that sex is a part of love. If you don't love someone, you shouldn't have sex with them. To me sex – I don't even like that word, I prefer 'making love' – is something beautiful. I get upset when it gets debased.'

'Is that violins I hear playing?' Tasha asks, cupping a hand to her ear.

Quentin comes to the rescue. 'No, leave her alone, Tash. She's allowed to express her view. Tell us more, Claire.'

'I don't like it when people use words like screwing or bonking, or even worse. It takes something which is essentially wonderful and makes it tacky. It's like putting a Monet in a garish plastic frame. And it puts all the emphasis on the *act*, as if that were more important than the relationship between the two people.'

'That's impossibly romantic, Claire,' opines Siobhàn, sharply. She stabs a new piece of bread with her fork to emphasize the point.

'What's more,' Claire continues, 'I believe intimacy makes you very vulnerable, and that you need some protection around it. So I still want to argue for marriage or a committed relationship as the best context for love-making. Otherwise you might be better with John's machine, or doing it on your own.'

'Masturbation? Is that what you're hinting at? A bit of digital manipulation?' Siobhàn watches Claire's grimace, and smiles. 'Hark the herald angel sings. I can't believe this – it's sooo last century.'

'Oh, blast!' exclaims Claire, removing her newly denuded fork from the fondue, and looking in vain for the piece of bread lost there.

'No exceptions, Claire,' Tasha pronounces with delight. She begins a slow handclap which is taken up by the others at the table.

Claire can hardly bring herself to look sideways. She is screwing up her paper napkin, wringing it in her hands. John has the beginnings of a slow smile on his face.

Bowing to the inevitable, Claire inclines her face towards John. To the astonishment of the spectators, she slides a hand behind John's head, and kisses him full and hard on the lips. The slow handclap erupts into enthusiastic applause. John's eyes open wide.

Siobhàn is scowling.

Claire withdraws, and there is a pink tinge to her cheeks. John stares at her momentarily, and reaches for his wine glass.

'Well,' says Quentin, 'I hope you both feel sufficiently chastised.'

'To get back to the subject,' Siobhàn intervenes, 'I just can't get my head around this commitment thing. Okay, maybe when it was tied to the pregnancy thing, then having a couple of people around for a while was a good idea. But why now? It's just a control mechanism, isn't it, marriage and heavy relationships and so on? Because we're all too scared to just enjoy sex for

> **The kiss originated when the first male reptile licked the first female reptile, implying in a subtle, complimentary way that she was as succulent as the small reptile he had for dinner the night before.**
> F. Scott Fitzgerald

> **Give me chastity and continence – but not yet.**
> Augustine of Hippo

its own sake. Generations of guilt still rattling around in our psyches. I mean it's just a physical pleasure, isn't it? Like having a good meal or a bath. You can enjoy without having to enter into some bloody contract.'

'To me, sex is a great disappointment,' offers Quentin, quietly.

'Say what?' asks Tasha.

'I've never once had a sexual encounter that's lived up to my expectations of it.'

'See me later,' says Siobhàn.

'Don't kid yourself. And I make a point of not sleeping with friends. But honestly, I'm with Claire on this one. Love is lovely. Relationship, the dance of engagement, the anticipation of knowledge – all of that gets sullied amidst the grunting and secretions.'

'Spoken like a true poet,' Tasha judges. 'But you're in fairyland, Quentin. You're in love with the idea of love. It's just a product, like any others. It sells flowers and keeps the marriage industry going, but it's a gigantic hoax. Real people do grunt and secrete. If you're going to love them then sex is part of it. I can't say I get enough of it to be an expert on the subject, but for me sex is somewhere in between Claire and Siobhàn.'

'Just what precisely,' grins Quentin, 'are you suggesting?'

'Sex has got to be more than a transaction,' declares John. 'People are sacred. They have

Love is two minutes
fifty-two seconds
of squishing noises.
It shows your mind
isn't clicking right.
Johnny Rotten

dignity. Whenever you start thinking about them in terms of commerce or what they're useful for, you devalue the whole human race.'

'Hullo, we're back to socialism again,' sneers Tasha.

'Crap,' John retorts. 'What I'm saying is that we need to get sexuality out of the arena of economics altogether.'

'Tell that to the prostitutes' collective!'

'Thanks for making my point for me. Sex as a transaction is prostitution. I would guess most of us see that as a tragedy. We hope for something better for ourselves.'

'There's this rich guy,' begins Quentin, 'sitting next to a beautiful woman at a dinner party. They get talking, and seem to be getting on fairly well. Part way through dessert, the guy whispers in her ear and asks her if she'll go to bed with him. "No way," she whispers back, "I'm married." She twists the wedding ring on her finger and flicks her eyes towards her husband sitting next to her on the other side. "What about if I gave you $500,000 for the one night?" our man persists. She stops and thinks about this. She knows he's got the money to spend. "Okay," she tells him. "How about for $100?" he asks her next. The woman is outraged. "Just what do you think I am?" she mutters angrily. "We've already established that," he says. "Now we're just haggling over the price."

· · · · · · · · ·

Sex is the great amateur art. The professional, male or female, is frowned upon; he or she misses the whole point and spoils the show.
David Cort

'So, John, you think sex should be in the context of a loving relationship, do you?' Siobhàn speaks with an edge to her voice.

'Yeah, I reckon that's the best place for it, in an ideal world.'

'This conviction would be a theoretical position, would it, then?' Her eyes are pure fire now. The undertones are clear to the others, who take a renewed interest in the fondue.

'We're not in an ideal world, Siobhàn,' explains John quietly.

'That we're not, John, that we're not. So, you bunch of Presbyterian butterfly-collectors, am I the only liberated one at the table?' she demands.

'If that's liberation, you can keep it,' Claire responds.

'I beg your bloody pardon, Miss Icebox from Chastity Square? Have you got something to say?'

'I'm sorry, Siobhàn, but let's be honest about it. You're perpetually in a mess with men. Your bedroom is like Piccadilly Circus. How many AIDS tests have you had now? And as soon as they're out of your bed you push them away in case they get close to you. If that's sophistication then I'm happy to stay naïve.'

There is a brief second's silence as the conversation's change of level is taken on board.

'My god, Claire,' utters Quentin in amazement, 'what did you have for breakfast?'

'My personal life has got nothing to do with you,' barks Siobhàn, recovering at last. 'What goes on in my bedroom is between me and whoever it goes on with.'

'Is it though?' John pries gently. 'Is sex just in the realm of privacy? Anything between consenting adults is okay? That's where we seem to have ended up leaving it as a society. But who controls the game? And who picks up the pieces?'

'What game?' Tasha asks, pleased to have the discussion back on less volatile ground.

'The game we're talking about. The negotiations and preconditions for sexual intimacy. The implications of a sexual encounter for the participants. The responsibility for any consequences like pregnancy or disease. It seems to me that things work better when everyone has a rough idea of what the rules are. But it's chaos out there at the moment. Okay, we ditched the old game plan and we're all very proud of ourselves for doing it. But what's to replace it? Confusion reigns. There's a hundred different expectations and most of us end up miserable because we can't quite get it right. If it's just down to what takes place behind the closed doors of a bedroom, then I can't see how we're ever going to get out of the mess we're in.'

'Hang on, I don't think we've all agreed that we're in such a mess yet,' cautions Quentin.

'No, he's right,' says Tasha. 'The brave new world is a cold place to be on a Saturday night. I'm going to speak for myself, all right? This is just me, my experience, and it doesn't mean anything for anyone else. What's more, if anyone

Losing my virginity was a career move.
Madonna

repeats this conversation outside of this room I'll personally disembowel them.'

'We get the picture,' acknowledges Quentin.

'What I'm looking for – me personally – is a bit of tenderness. I like sex, I've had some rollicking good times, and my boundaries are reasonably loose. But after it's all over, I want someone who will lie there with their arm around me and talk about something important. Listen to me, share some secrets, tell me things I want to hear. If I had to choose between relationship with no sex and sex with no relationship, I'd go for the relationship every time. Well, most of the time.'

'Me too,' says Claire. 'Why is it so hard to find? What's happened to love, as in putting your own needs aside in order to concentrate on the other person?'

'Save us,' Siobhàn implores. 'Next we'll be advocating virginity – keeping ourselves for the big night. I feel like I'm in a time capsule. This is the dawn of the new millennium, you know? If you're all so committed to the asexual life, I'd have to say from observation that you're non-practising. As for me, I'll take sex without relationship every time. In fact I can't think of when I've shared love and sex in the same bed.' And she is looking directly at John.

'Siobhàn darling, I think you're being naïve if you're suggesting that it's all on the level of bodily functions,' Quentin chips in. 'We're much more complex than that. We have emotions and dreams and hearts and souls. You can't treat your body like some disengaged shell that can be pitched into battle to find a little pleasure for you.'

'Why not?'

'Because like it or not, your body is part of you. What you do with it affects the whole of you.'

'No arguments, but what's the point?'

'The point is that it has an effect emotionally and spiritually whenever you – or I or anyone else – has a sexual relationship with another human being.'

'Nah, I'm not wearing this spiritual stuff. A bonk is a bonk is a bloody good time. If you make sex into something sacred it's no wonder you get disappointed with it. I have low expectations and so I usually have a good time.'

'What about loneliness, then?' Quentin asks.

'Where are we going now?' Tasha enquires.

'There's something at the core of us that sex on its own never quite touches,' says Quentin. 'You can be at it like a rabbit every waking moment, and still be desperately lonely at the same time. I would say that a lot of sex is like morphine – it's a pain-blocker. We use it to stop the ache inside of us. But the hunger goes a lot deeper than sex can ever reach. It's a hunger for love. Okay, I'll personalize it. I'm hungry for love.'

Despite herself, Siobhàn reaches across the table to take his hand and hold it.

'A story,' John begins. 'There's a man who's searching for something real in life. He's open to

We have hearts within,
Warm, live, improvident,
indecent hearts.
Elizabeth Barrett Browning

For me, the highest
level of sexual
excitement is in
a monogamous
relationship.
Warren Beatty

all possibilities, but he's not gullible. He is determined to doubt everything, and only hold on to that which stands up to scrutiny. To save himself from compromise, he vows that he won't enter into any commitments or contracts which might blur his objectivity. He searches the world, far and wide, looking for something – not even sure quite what. There's some promising leads, but every time he thinks he's about to touch his holy grail, the ground collapses under his feet and confirms his cynicism.

'Eventually he retreats into a remote area to dream and meditate. He's staying in a farm cottage, and the farmer, save us from stereotypes, has a daughter. She is, of course, beautiful. Her main joys in life are roaming the hills and weaving great colourful bolts of fabric. The man meets her in the fields and strikes up a friendship. She shows him her weaving; he talks to her of his quest. As you do, they fall in love. They spend more and more time together. For the first time in many years, the man becomes truly happy. He senses he is on the brink of discovery.

'He wants to take her to bed, to take their relationship to the heights and depths of potential. But her father is very strict, and it's a conservative rural area. She won't sleep with him unless they're married. The man is sorely tempted, but he can't bring himself to break his vow of objectivity. And so he has to cut the ties and leave, the relationship unconsummated. Something inside of him dies and, naturally, for

I think a lot of people are so afraid of making a mistake that they make the biggest mistake of all: they don't live.

T-Bone Burnett

the rest of his life, he remains searching and unfulfilled. On his deathbed he comforts himself that he has been true to his principles. But in his imagination he still sees the woman he loves, and grieves.'

John falls silent. The others look on in anticipation. Siobhàn has her eyes closed.

'That's it?' asks Tasha.

'Sorry, yes, that's it.'

'Not much of a story, was it?'

But Siobhàn has her eyes open again.

'What was her name?' she asks.

'Belinda,' says John.

'Have I missed something?' asks Claire.

'Oops,' cries Siobhàn. Despite fishing in the bowl, her bread is gone.

'This'll be interesting,' says Quentin, noting that Tasha is sitting on Siobhàn's right.

But Siobhàn is not at all self-conscious. She reaches across before Tasha has had time to work out the implications, and kisses her on the lips. Tasha initially draws her head back in fright, but Siobhàn pursues her and holds the kiss for some seconds. Applause follows. Tasha is bright red and breathing heavily.

'Are you sure that wasn't a deliberate drop?' asks Quentin.

'Absolutely innocent,' says Siobhàn. 'Now, what are we going to sort out next week?'

> **We are never so defenceless against suffering as when we love, never so helplessly unhappy as when we have lost our loved object or its love.**
>
> Sigmund Freud

Chapter Four

'Gender,' says Tasha, peering through the haze. Grilling the mussels was a good idea, but the smoke suggests they might have been a fraction close to the element.

The one word stops conversation dead at the table. Puzzled eyes are trained upon her.

'What d'you mean, gender?' Siobhàn is bold enough to ask. 'What's to discuss?'

'Shit!' exclaims Tasha, dropping the hot tray onto the bench. She hates cooking, and the feeling is mutual. 'Sorry. What I was thinking of was following on a bit from last week. Thinking about sexual identity – you know, the sort of gay/bi/ straight thing, and whatever other options there are that I haven't heard about yet. Any objections? It's my call anyway. If I'm going to do the firking cooking then I get to pick the topic.'

'Nothing personal in this, is there, Tash?' Quentin asks.

'Piss off,' she growls, and it's difficult to say whether it's the heat of the kitchen or something else which has made her face red.

'Before we start,' Claire interjects, 'there's something I wanted to talk about. Is that all right?'

'Go for it,' Siobhàn interprets the mouth-filled nods from the others.

> Men should be saying 'I want to become a woman.' The world would be a far better place if more men wanted to become women, than women wanted to become men.
>
> Albert Halsey

66

'It's about you, Siobhàn. Last Friday night I said some awful things about you here, and I've felt guilty about it all week. I don't know if it was the wine — but I had no right to judge your personal life and I'm deeply sorry for doing it. I was rude and tactless and I apologize. There. I wanted to say that in front of everyone.'

'Ah bollocks, Claire. I mean thanks and all that but I can hardly remember what you said. My skin's fairly well thick by now, and I've been called a lot worse by people I liked a lot less. Don't fret about it.' She smiles at Claire with millennia of Irish welcome.

Claire swallows hard. 'I think I might have been a little defensive, you see. I've been thinking about it ever since. These Friday nights are horrible — I keep going over the conversation afterwards. I suspect some of my own personal issues might have been coming through in my reactions.'

'Oooh, gossip,' says Quentin. 'Do tell, darling.'

John frowns at him and Siobhàn scowls. Tasha is sucking her burned fingers.

'No, it's all right,' responds Claire. 'I think I do want to tell. I've lived with it on my own for a long time. It was when I was still living at home up in Cheltenham. I was doing very well — good marks at school, the right circle of friends, plenty of money. My parents were pleased enough, as much as they let on. They were going through a rough patch, with Daddy away from home so often. Mummy began spending a lot of time with her art tutor, who was a rather gorgeous Italian. I

Peace between neighbours,
Peace between kindred,
Peace between lovers,
In love of the King of life.
Gaelic blessing

67

began to wonder if she was having an affair with him, though I couldn't bring myself to contemplate my mother doing that sort of thing.

'I was at a party at a friend's place. I must have been seventeen. I had a crush on a boy who was there, but by the end of the evening he had paired up with another girl. I must have been feeling a bit melancholy. Late at night I pitched in and helped starting to clear up glasses and things. I ended up in the kitchen, doing dishes with my girlfriend's father. I'm not sure what we chatted about, but he seemed friendly enough. He offered to drive me home, which suited me as I didn't have a car. It was a few miles to my place, across the countryside.

'It was a night with a full moon, in late summer. As we came over the crest of a hill, you could see across this magnificent Cotswolds countryside. It seemed to be lit up with the softest of glows. It was so beautiful that I cried out, and my friend's father, Brian, stopped the car so that we could get out and look.'

'Claire, this is so predictable,' Siobhàn moans.

'I suppose it is,' Claire continues. 'Though not to me at the time; I was hopelessly innocent. I can still see the moonlight on those hills. Brian asked me what I wanted most from life, and I prattled on. He talked about his sense of disappointment — how he'd started off with dreams and had to settle for much less. His marriage was on the rocks, he wasn't sleeping with his wife anymore. We talked about music and books and poetry. He was a perfect gentleman. At one stage while we were

It is important to tell, at least from time to time, the secret of who we truly and fully are — even if we tell it only to ourselves — because otherwise we run the risk of losing track of who we truly and fully are and little by little come to accept instead the highly edited version which we put forth in hope that the world will find it more acceptable than the real thing.

Frederick Buechner

chatting, he reached out and stroked my hair. But it was so natural and caring that I hardly noticed.

'We must have stayed up there for an hour. Nothing happened, and eventually he drove me home. But when I got into bed I felt so brimful of life and wonder. It seemed to me that Brian was terribly wise, and I felt desperately sad for him that he was unhappy. So when he rang later in the week and asked me out for a coffee, I was glad to see him. As Siobhàn says, it was predictable. Within two weeks we were sleeping together. It all happened so quickly, and suddenly there we were making love on a blanket out in the countryside. Of course it became a regular thing, and I grew to enjoy it. Brian was so tender and loving, and I was pleased to be making him happy.

'Keeping it secret was all part of the fun at first. Later on I wanted everyone to know, and started pushing Brian to be more and more reckless. We began sneaking home to his place during the day, when there was no one at home. Brian was in law, so he had a lot of freedom to come and go. One day, his daughter, my friend Sandra, came home unexpectedly. We weren't in bed, thank God, but we were having a cup of tea in the lounge, listening to some music. I made some lame excuse about borrowing a record, but naturally Sandra guessed straight away. She was absolutely disgusted.

'All hell broke loose after that. Brian's wife found out, and she rang my parents. I came home one afternoon and there they were waiting for me with ashen faces. They couldn't bring themselves

We promise according to our hopes, and perform according to our fears.
La Rochefoucauld

to talk about it directly. Mummy just said she was terribly disappointed, and started crying, and Daddy banged on about going to see a doctor to make sure I wasn't in trouble. We still haven't broached the subject in any obvious way. Only innuendoes. I think my father has despised me ever since that day. And now that I've become a "shop-girl", as he calls me, he can hardly even be civil.

'Brian's marriage broke up. I was hopeful when I first heard, but of course the whole relationship had become intensely embarrassing for him. He ended up marrying a woman from his office, and went on to become a judge in the Family Court. I see his name in the paper now and again. I became a girl with a "reputation", and life became hell for me. I gave up school and took off from home for London. I couldn't get out of the place fast enough.

'But whatever I think of Brian now, he gave me an introduction to sexual experience that was very loving. When I got up to London, I had a few brief flings which gave me a taste of how *mean* sex can be when that's all there is to it. But I do recognize that some of my attitudes may be mixed up with all the shame and regret of my encounter with Brian. It's hard to separate it all out.'

'Ah Claire, you big bunny, you're so... Claireish,' Siobhàn grins. 'Don't be apologizing for getting hurt along the way.'

'That was brave to trust us with that, Claire,' says John seriously.

'Spare us your namby-pamby social work bullshit,' complains Tasha. 'And besides, I want us

Social work
is a band-aid on
the festering wounds
of society.
Alexander Chase

to get on to my topic. You don't mind, do you, Claire?'

But Claire is looking into the distance.

'Sausages?' asks Quentin, in astonishment.

'Devilled sausages, if you don't mind,' counters Tasha, staring him down. 'Any complaints?'

'None at all,' mutters Quentin. 'Looks lovely. And rice too.'

'I never claimed to be a cook. Take it or leave it.'

'Tell us about this topic of yours, Tasha,' John steps in. 'Where do you want us to start?'

'Okay, but no more about the food or I'll start throwing it at someone. And my glass is empty. I saw that bit in the paper this week about some fundamentalist group protesting outside the Gay & Lesbian Ball. They looked like the usual sort of nutters. One of them was carrying a placard which said "God hates faggots". There was a picture of a protester arguing with a good-looking guy in a tux. They were screaming at each other – looked for all the world like two dogs ready for a fight. Neither of them was listening to the other. I can't help wondering what all the angst is that drives the whole thing.'

'The problem with this one is going to be getting a bit of opposition,' says John.

'How do you mean?' asks Siobhàn.

'We all feel the same way, don't we? The protesters are miserable homophobic bigots, and the partygoers are people trying to get on with their lives without any hassle.'

> **The mind of a bigot is like the pupil of the eye; the more light you pour on it, the more it will contract.**
> Oliver Wendell Holmes

'Look, I haven't finished yet,' retorts Tasha. 'You're right – we can all compete with each other to see who's the most PC in the room. But I want to dig deeper. Last week, when Siobhàn kissed me – and it was lovely, Siobhàn, truly it was – I had this instant bad reaction thing. Now it might have been the same reaction if Quentin had reached over and kissed me...'

'Sweetheart – shall we try?' jibes Quentin.

'... but I suspect there was some gut-level reaction against the girl on girl thing. And I remember a few years back, watching this full-on scene between two guys in a film, and squirming in my seat. It was like I was watching someone pull the wings off flies. And so, I don't know what. Am I just a homophobe? Where does the energy come from for this anti stuff?'

'Maybe it's just not your scene,' says Quentin. 'I hate sport, but I can't say I've ever considered myself to have a phobia about it. You can be turned off something without it meaning you're a bigot.'

Siobhàn has a glint in her eye. 'On the other hand,' she ponders, 'it could be because deep down you really like it, Tash. Maybe that kiss awoke your baser passions. Maybe your reaction is because you're scared of what you might unleash if you let yourself go.'

'Mmmm... maybe. But how deep do I have to go to know what I like and what I don't like? Is there someone inside of me, a secret dike, trying to get out? It's possible, you know, but if she's there I've never met her. It's kind of scary to think that "I" might not be "I"; that I don't know who I am.'

'You don't have to answer this,' Siobhàn continues for the prosecution, 'but have you ever swung the other way?'

Claire covers her eyes with her hands.

'Nothing serious,' says Tasha, 'just the usual schoolgirl stuff.'

'And what would that amount to?'

'A few dreamy kisses with a girlfriend who was staying the night. A couple of times we might have taken each other through to orgasm. But nothing regular, and not to the stage of dildos or vibrators.'

'How was it?' Siobhàn demands.

'It was okay. Sort of friendly and intimate. I didn't have much to compare it with at the time. But I've never felt a huge lust after women. I don't think I'm a repressed lesbian.'

John joins in. 'I can't see that being hetero makes you automatically homophobic, any more than being gay makes you heterophobic. Is there such a word, heterophobic? I don't think there is.'

'Any closet-exiters among us? Come out, come out, wherever you are. How about you, Quentin?' Siobhàn turns to face him.

'You don't give up, do you, chook? I wouldn't mind a fiver for every time I've been asked if I'm gay. How could I be gay when I'm so in love with women? I love you all, you beautiful creatures.'

'When was the last time you were in an actual

I just wish more of my fellow queers would come out sometimes. It's nice out here, you know?
Elton John

relationship with one of these creatures, then?' Siobhàn insists.

'It depends what you mean by relationship, darling.'

'I mean one in which the woman you love actually has some feelings towards you as well – a relationship where there's two people relating to each other, instead of one mad lovesick bastard baying at the moon.'

'No, Siobhàn; be absolutely direct. I insist. Stop holding back.'

'Look, Quentin, it's a fact. Every week you come home from the writers' group head over heels with a different woman. But as far as I know, you've never asked any of them out.'

'I asked Maureen,' Quentin says defensively. 'But she turned out to be married.'

'But that's ideal, isn't it? That's what you're looking for. Your prime requirement in a woman is that she be unavailable. Then you can write poems about how miserable you are. Loving ideal women could be an easy alternative for you instead of loving a man.'

'We could be drifting here,' John warns. 'I'm not sure we should be playing "spot the gay". What about sexual orientation itself? Where does it come from? Are people born with it, or does it develop over time?'

'If your mummy made you a homosexual, could she make me one too? Sorry,' adds Quentin, unbowed by his inquisition.

The human sex drive is extraordinarily powerful. It may become inappropriately affixed to underwear, corpses, animals, children, footstools and members of the same sex.
Jerry Shultz

74

'It's got to be there at birth, hasn't it?' asks Claire, who has floated back to the present. 'I mean at least the leaning that way. Otherwise why would anyone bother?'

'There's this interesting case,' says John, 'I read about in one of the journals at work. A seven-month-old baby was getting some surgical work done, and there was this accident where his penis got sliced off. The parents consulted with doctors and decided to have his gender reassigned to female, with a bit of medical assistance. So at the age of seventeen months, they performed surgery to give him female genitals, changed his name and started dressing him in girl's clothes. He grew up a pretty normal girl, whatever that means. What made the case really interesting was that he was an identical twin, and his brother was raised as a boy all the way through. So you've got two kids with identical genes, but different social conditioning, and they turn out as different genders.'

'So what are you saying? That sexual orientation is all conditioning?' Siobhàn demands.

'I'm not saying anything. I'm just telling a story.'

'How come no one asks what makes a person hetero?' Quentin asks.

'That's because being heterosexual is considered as normal,' Claire informs. 'You don't have to justify normality.'

'Precisely,' Quentin pronounces, to Claire's puzzlement.

'It's not like people are one thing or another all

God bless the lost, the confused, the unsure, the bewildered, the puzzled, the mystified, the baffled and the perplexed.
Michael Leunig

their life, anyway,' Tasha insists. 'People might start out straight and go gay, or be bi or whatever. The same person can be different things at different times in their life.'

'I'm not so sure about all that,' worries John.

'What's there to be not sure about?' Quentin wants to know.

'A person might be gay or lesbian, I can accept that. Okay, so for whatever reason, they've got a built-in predilection towards members of their own sex. But when you start talking about it sliding around all over the place, I get nervous. You start to put it in the realm of fashion or whim, as if people can just reinvent their sexual identity whenever they like.'

'And can't they?' continues Quentin.

'What worries me is that you start treating the whole thing too casually. A partner becomes whatever you fancy according to your monthly preference. We're getting back to our earlier discussion here, but I want to treat love and sexuality more seriously than that.'

'So you're discounting the possibility of bisexuality?' Siobhàn asks in wonder.

'You're pushing me further than I want to go,' John counters.

'Is that sexual harassment?' smirks Quentin.

John pulls a face in response. 'I'm saying that I'm unhappy about sexual identity falling into the realm of style. I don't think it's as trivial as "whatever I feel like this week". It's become a hell of a lot more trendy to be gay than straight. What

The Bible contains six admonishments to homosexuals and 362 admonishments to heterosexuals. That doesn't mean God doesn't love heterosexuals. It's just that they need more supervision.

Lynne Lavner

happens to people if they cross the lines just to be part of the in-group?'

'You tell us, John. What does happen?' Siobhàn asks with an air of incredulity.

'It buggers them up,' John decides.

'I sometimes wonder if my father was gay,' says Tasha. 'I never really knew him. The bastard died on me when I was five years old. It could have been because of living with an alcoholic – that'd be enough to make anyone see death as a way out. But mum's always made sneering remarks at him. She used to talk about "that pansy, your father". One Christmas time when I was about thirteen, I interrogated my uncle, my father's brother. He never let on much, apart from the fact that my father wasn't really a *man's* man, and that he'd advised my father against marrying my mother.

'Apparently when he was little my father used to spend all his time drawing pictures, and by all accounts was quite good at it. Then one day he got crayon on the carpet, and his mother threw out all his drawing stuff, and made a rule that he couldn't do any artwork in the house. He used to get beaten if he was found with a drawing in his schoolbook. My uncle described him as intense. Too much worried about his inner life, he said, a waste of bloody time. If he had just got on with things, he might still be here today, my uncle said.

You use a glass mirror to see your face; you use works of art to see your soul.
George Bernard Shaw

'I sometimes wonder,' John muses, 'if anyone can do anything wrong anymore.'

'That's got to be the mother of all generalizations,' argues Quentin. 'You're going to have to tell us what you mean, John-boy.'

'Okay, but I'm treading on thin ice here so don't push me in.' He takes a swig of red wine and throws his hair back off his face before continuing. 'In my parents' generation, things were right or wrong, and most people agreed about it. Whether it came from the Bible or social conditioning or whatever, most folks would have happily told you that "homosexuality" was wrong. So nowadays we all understand that point of view as being hopelessly prejudiced, and a means of marginalizing people who didn't fit in the mainstream of society.

'But the way we've done it is by redefining our terms, yeah? Homosexual has become gay, ardent heteros have become homophobes or latent gays, good has been equated with tolerant. I'm not knocking it, so don't start throwing stones yet. But if our age of superior understanding can redefine what used be wrong, and make it acceptable, what's to stop it happening everywhere?'

Siobhàn is looking puzzled. 'I still can't see where this is going,' she says.

'Let's take the case of adults having sex with children, what used to be called paedophilia. I don't want to assume too much, but I would guess most of us around the table would still consider that to be wrong.'

'It's the main bloody industry of the church where I come from,' mutters Siobhàn.

'But maybe that's just a matter of perspective. There was this guy in New Zealand who set up a community based around the idea that society was screwed up on sex. He argued that most of our conventions about sexuality and who could do what to whom were based on thousands of years of social conditioning. Now, in these days of enlightenment, we have the opportunity of freeing sexuality up from all the constraints and hangups foisted on us by our forebears. So he encouraged free expression of sexual impulses within the community. Group sex, partner-swapping, whatever. Children were encouraged to watch the adults at it. All in the name of liberation.

'So then the children want to join in on the sex, you see. Kids want to be in on anything the adults are doing. And the leader of the community sees this as fantastic. See what happens, he says, when you remove the barriers. These children are doing what comes naturally. We need to encourage them to explore their sexuality. Now a few years later, some of these kids grow up and leave the community. They talk to other people about what has happened, and end up going to the police with charges of sexual abuse. The community leader is hauled into court. He admits what took place, but denies that there was anything wrong with it.'

'What happened?' Claire asks.

'He got convicted and put in prison. But here's the point: how do we know he's not right, and that we're still at a repressed stage of our sexual evolution?'

If any of you put a stumbling block before one of these little ones who believe in me, it would be better for you if a great millstone were fastened around your neck and you were drowned in the depth of the sea.

Jesus

'It's the power thing that makes it wrong,' Siobhàn suggests. 'There's an imbalance of power between adults and children. So any sexual relationship is always potentially abusive.'

'I can't believe anyone can even imagine that children should be encouraged into sexual experience,' says Claire. 'They're not in a position to be able to evaluate the consequences, or know what's right or wrong.'

'How old were you when you struck up with Brian?' inquires Quentin. 'Seventeen? I bet you thought you were old enough to make your own decisions. And the age of sexual maturity is getting lower and lower, isn't it?'

'You see, you get to the stage where you can justify anything,' John asserts. 'There are paedophilia groups now which go by such titles as the Man Boy Love Association. These guys see themselves as simply having a love for young people which has a sexual dimension. They claim that their interest in children is the equivalent of sexual orientation, and that they have a perfect right to exercise it the same as anyone else.'

'Hang on,' Siobhàn jumps in. 'Aren't we getting dangerously close to associating homosexuality with paedophilia here?'

'Yeah, I'm sorry – I don't want to make that connection,' John answers. 'What I'm saying is that once you start reinterpreting what's right and wrong, it becomes more and more difficult to draw a line anywhere.'

One must remember that both wild things and men are animals, but wild things are not people.

Helen Hoover

'How about zoophilia?' asks Tasha.

'It's non-contagious,' Siobhàn responds.

'I don't know what you're talking about,' Claire pleads.

'Bestiality is the traditional word for it,' explains Siobhàn, 'but it's such a beastly word.'

'Zoophilia is the sanitized version,' continues Tasha. 'It means love of animals, which some people take very seriously.'

'Well it's okay by me,' says Quentin, 'so long as the animal consents.'

'Whatever happened to good old perversion?' Claire wails.

'My point exactly,' John rejoices. 'Perversion has been redefined. Nothing is wrong any more, though the odd bit of behaviour may still be termed inappropriate.'

'You're sounding a trifle revisionist for a wanky liberal,' remarks Tasha.

'Maybe you were a bit quick to catalogue me.'

'What I want to know,' demands Siobhàn, 'is how we started talking off talking about sexual orientation and ended up with farmers screwing sheep. Or is that a prominent topic of conversation in the Antipodes?'

> It is better to be old-fashioned and right than to be up-to-date and wrong.
> Tiorio

A round of sheep jokes marks the transition to dessert. Claire complains but laughs with the rest of them. Tasha produces a cherry torte, purchased from the delicatessen. Around the table there is a sense of connection, which none of them can name. It is as if all the colours were brighter, the wine softer, the people closer.

'I did fall in love with a boy once,' Quentin confesses in a moment of quiet.

'Tell, tell,' encourages Siobhàn.

'He was a year ahead of me at school. He sang in the school choir, and he was gorgeous. I couldn't get through Assembly without swooning. Geoffrey, his name was. Tall and thin, with very pale skin and lank black hair. His eyes were black; I'm sure they were. A few times he was a soloist, and I would have tears streaming down my face listening to him. I used to write poems about him. He didn't even know I existed, I don't think. He was on the other side of that great social divide between forms. Time passed, and I got over him. I still have the poems somewhere.'

'Oh god. More unrequited love,' groans Tasha.

'I thought you said you weren't gay,' Siobhàn points out.

'I don't consider that I am,' claims Quentin. 'It was just a vortex of adolescent emotion, which could have attached itself to anything. The fact that I was at a boys' school meant that it attached itself to a boy rather than a girl. It might have alighted on a sheep in a different context, I suppose. But I never acted on the impulse, and I don't see it as having any defining significance for my orientation.'

'But you have at least experienced love or attraction for someone of your own gender?' John insists.

'Who hasn't? Come on, all of you, be honest. Is there anyone here who can truthfully say that you've never had any romantic or sexual attraction towards someone who happened to have the same bits as you?'

There are a few seconds of stunned silence as the congregation searches individual memory banks.

'I thought not,' Quentin interprets the quiet. 'So let's drop the pretence and the defensiveness, shall we?'

'I actually think that's why it's such a hot issue,' says Siobhàn. 'It's that we see the tendencies within us, and we're scared to face up to them.'

'So we demonize what's inside of us that we don't like,' John adds. 'You could be right. I'm always a bit uncomfortable around people who are violently against anything – it makes me wonder what's going on inside.'

'I did a short story along those lines,' says Quentin.

'It was set in the Middle Ages, during the time of a plague. This particular village has managed to stay clear of it, while all around them other towns are laid waste. Every morning they go out into the fields and they can smell the stench of bodies burning on the wind. The villagers consider themselves to be blessed by God to escape the disease, and they go every day to the church in the centre of the town to pray to God that their

My wife is not a lesbian and neither is my son. I've never had sex with a man and neither has my wife.
Letter to Lavendar
Network Newspaper

health may be preserved. The village priest is a canny old man, and while he acknowledges the mercy of God, he's also careful about who comes and goes to the settlement, wary in case there should be a plague carrier among them.

'One day a woman arrives at the town gate, and begs to be let in. She tells the story of having been taken into captivity by a wandering group of monks and nuns, and forced to participate in their dubious religious practices. Now she's escaped, and is seeking refuge in the village. The priest is summoned. He interviews her and inspects her. Her story seems genuine, and she looks to be in good health. In fact, she's not only attractive but vaguely familiar. The woman has some gold coins which she offers to donate to the church, and the priest decides to admit her.

'He takes her back to the church to question her further. She tells him of the group of nomadic preachers that have held her prisoner for some months. The priest is very interested in the village of her origin. He knows it well, and feels a stirring in his loins as he recalls his days there as a young priest. It was the time of his greatest power, but also the time of his downfall. He fell in love with a beautiful woman of Arabic blood, and ended up in a state of sin with her. His bishop had intervened to hush it up and have him removed. Nevertheless, the taste of the woman's flesh has always stayed with the priest, and he recalls it as he talks to this stranger.

'Some days after her arrival in the village, there

is a commotion. When the priest arrives, he recognizes instantly the signs of the dreaded plague. He curses his stupidity and prays that it's not too late. The body of the dead man is dragged outside into the fields, and placed on a pile of wood. In the middle of it is erected a pole, and the priest leads the woman stranger, the plague-carrier, out to it. She's tied to the pole, and the fire lit. The priest stands guard over it. As the woman burns, the flames for a moment frame her face, and light it in a special way. In an instant, he recognizes her. Looking out at him is the woman he loved so many years ago. With great sadness, he realizes he has just burned his daughter.

'He leads the village in fervent prayer, calling them all to mass. But one by one the deaths start, and the plague takes hold. The entire village is eventually wiped out; no one is spared. Which is not surprising, because, of course, the priest is the plague carrier.

'That's the story,' says Quentin. 'I'm not sure what it's about.'

> **To betray you must first belong.**
> Harold Philby

Chapter Five

John retreats to the back doorstep for a smoke. He leans against the doorframe and inhales deeply. The clouds are urban orange, with no sign of stars. Lorries relieve themselves in the distance, and the air is tainted with diesel. Siobhàn wanders out and squeezes in beside him.

'Smoke?' he offers.

'T'anks,' says Siobhàn. She concentrates on rolling the cigarette.

'The sky's too low,' growls John.

'Same height as it's ever been,' responds Siobhàn. 'High enough so's you don't bang your head on it and close enough to send rain.'

'Where I grew up, the sky is miles high. On a fine day you can't see the end of it. It's amazing. And blue — there's nothing like it over here. You have to see it to believe it. As a boy I used to lie on my back and look up trying to see where it finished and where outer space began. Then at night the stars would come out in their millions. Magic.'

'Don't be telling me your tales of wonder, John. In my land we don't look up for fear of getting rain in our eyes. And some bastard's likely to steal your Guinness while you're not watching.'

'When you live under a high sky, it seems like anything is possible. You can take on the world, you know? The whole of life is open-ended.'

The golden moments in the stream of life rush past us, and we see nothing but sand; the angels come to visit us, and we only know them when they are gone.

P.L. Debevoise

'I wish I knew what it was you're talking about.
I grew up with the priests rabbiting on about God
and his vengeance. The sky was where God lived,
so it was none of my business to be looking up.
Better to keep your head down and get on with
living, and hope that God took no notice of you.
The whole of Ireland would rather be looking at
peat than stars. Unless of course you're a woman,
in which case you have your arse on the peat and
your face full of stars a fair part of the time.'

'Tell me about growing up.'

'Ah, I didn't grow up at all. But I was third of
six children. My people were Catholic right
enough, good working-class stock. My Da was a
brickie. He worked long hours when he had the
work, and drank even longer hours. My Ma spent
her time churning out sprogs until she got sick of
it, and went on the pill. The priest told her it was
a mortal sin, and she told him to try shitting
bowling balls and then he could tell her what was
a sin and what wasn't. It wasn't such a bad life, in
Dublin. We were always poor, but there was a lot
of fun to be had. Always the people and the crack,
and some reason to be celebrating.'

'I can't imagine you as a child. Tell me a story.'

'We'll make an Irishman of you yet. All right,
let me think now. There was my first communion.
D'you know what that is? It's a big ceremony
when you take communion for the first time. I
was ten, and it was the biggest event of my life.
You have to wear a white dress for it, see, only we
didn't have the money for it. I hated wearing

**If God lived on earth,
people would break
his windows.**
Jewish Proverb

87

dresses anyway, but my Ma insisted. So we borrowed one off my cousin. I put it on and had my hair done up and I was parading around like a little princess. Well the boys next door, see, they saw me in it and laughed themselves silly. They started calling me names and that. One thing led to another, and soon enough we were rolling around on the ground trading punches.

'The dress got torn and dirty, and there was blood on it. I kept trying to tell my Ma that it wasn't my blood. I thought she'd be proud of me, but she just kept yelling that it soon would be. There was a crisis meeting and my Da found some money he'd been hiding and persuaded the man from the dress shop to open. There was nothing in my size so we got the nearest we could. I had no bruises and I scrubbed up pretty well. So we arrive at the church with everything sorted, and looking good. Except that in my rush to get ready, I'd forgotten to put knickers on. I had this big petticoat so it didn't matter too much.

'Everything was going well, and the bishop was there and all to do the ceremony. There was a group of us, and we were processing up the aisle with the boys on one side and the girls on the other. Halfway up, the boy next to me stuck out his foot and tripped me up. I may have put chewing gum in his hair the week before or something – I can't say I recall. So there I go, head over heels, and end up in a sprawling heap on the floor. The girl behind tries to give me a hand up, but all she succeeds in doing is lifting my dress so that my bare bum is showing to all the church. It still gets talked about in the parish. I'm the girl who mooned the bishop.'

'Was it something you believed in, the church and all that?'

'That's a Protestant sort of a question, now, John. Amongst the Catholics you don't so much believe in the church as belong to it. It's a total culture sort of thing, you know? It's the air you breathe and the ground you stand on. I've never been able to get enough distance from it to have an opinion, but I don't go to church anymore.'

'Why not?'

'It's got nothing to do with me, nor I with it. After my first communion, I signed a pledge to say I wouldn't drink until I was twenty-one. Here's me, a ten-year-old, making promises more than I know what they mean. When I was fifteen, a group of us drank a bottle of vodka and I ended up screwing the son of the local constable down in the railway yards. It was the start of a separation between how I was living and what was going on at church. But I'm as much Catholic as I am Irish, even though I don't go to church. How about you?'

'I grew up in a land where the only sacred place was the rugby field, and Colin Meads was Christ.'

'Colin who?'

'Colin Meads. A giant of a man – he was a lock for the All Blacks. He was a back-country farmer who never spoke much and certainly showed no emotions. In a test against South Africa, he broke his hand in the first half, but kept playing right

The churches are finished; we don't have a pow-wow, a place to be emotional. The closest we get to that is a really great concert.

Annie Lennox

Can you imagine how it feels to believe in Christ and be so uncomfortable with Christianity? The church is an empty, hollow building.

Bono

through the game. He did it for us, you see. Bore pain so that we could win the rugby. That's the only sort of salvation we have time for in the Antipodes.'

There is a silence as John deviates into the interior. Siobhàn is content to sit and wait. She knows there is some secret buried there. It will find its time and place to come out.

Tasha stares at the screen. She's in the tunnel, a place where no one can find her. It's a cavern with its mouth somewhere between her eyes and the VDU. Once she enters this cyber-cavern, there is no further communication with the outside world. It's where she works; where she is creator, brooding over the chaos. She's come to love the tunnel, and prefers it in many ways to life outside.

Today, however, it's not the skeletal structures of code that she's confronting, but unsummoned memories. Cleaning up the vomit and putting her mother to bed. Keeping the boys quiet in the morning and getting them off to school. Coming home at the end of the day to an empty house.

There was a maths teacher, Mr Pattison. He was an old man with a kind face. Often he would talk to me after class. Nothing special, just chit-chat. Asking how I was. He must have known, she now realizes. Must have understood that I was the child of an alcoholic; an at-risk child. Spent time with me working on my maths. Made it come alive.

It was my escape. A world I could slip into where all problems had solutions. A clean clinical

What would life be without arithmetic, but a scene of horrors?

Sydney Smith

existence where logic reigned. Crisp numbers without cant or ambiguity. Always predictable, always safe. With numbers I could create; could control my destiny. It was always a way out, a hiding place from that stinking bitch of a mother. And it worked. I'm free, almost.

'... she looked up, and saw him watching. Then she knew that it would soon be starting all over again.'

Pamela finishes her story, looking around at other members of the group in hopeful anticipation. Most of them are looking down. The story is lame and predictable and overly sentimental.

'Your beginnings are much better,' says Quentin brightly.

She smiles coyly at him. Quentin could stand an acre of her shocking prose for the sake of one of those smiles. Pamela is forty, with dark hair and a wide smile. She is of the age which Quentin adores, with full ripe ease of womanhood. So much more attractive than the china-doll beauty promoted in fashion magazines.

'I wondered if you might fill out the male character a little,' offers Edna tentatively.

Edna is a published short-story writer, and so has considerable sway within the group. She has steel-grey hair which she has kept long and wears tied back from her face. In her mid-fifties, she is happily married. This does not stop Quentin from admiring and flirting with her. Edna is glad of the attention.

Flattery is all right – if you don't inhale.
Adlai Stevenson

'What do you mean?' asks Pamela, defensive and hurt.

'You've done so well with rounding out the woman's character,' suggests Edna with kindness and not a little dishonesty, 'that the man seems a trifle pale by comparison. I'm not sure I've got to know him apart from his physical description. But very promising, just the same. Now, I'm sure Quentin will have something to read us this week.'

And Quentin, rummaging in his bag, may well have a few lines to read.

John had wormed his way out of the cooking cycle with threats of baked beans, and a desperate argument that he'd contributed by arriving. Not that I mind preparing food, thinks Claire, but it's the thought of coming up with some beastly topic of conversation. Like zoophilia, she grins, despite herself.

The meal, like Claire herself, is beautiful and carefully presented. She begins with crumbed fillets of aubergine and camembert, with a sweet cranberry sauce. It is accompanied by slices of melon. For the main course she has decided on lamb d'ambruzzio, with grilled mushrooms and sautéed potatoes. Dessert is pavlova with kiwifruit, in honour of John.

'Come on, Claire, stop holding out on us,' pleads Siobhàn. 'What are we going to be talking about tonight?'

'Hasn't anyone else got something they want to discuss?' groans Claire.

'Your turn, most beautiful Claire. The cook must decide.' Quentin is determined.

'Oh, all right. The topic I thought we could start to look at... it's not really anything deep like we've been talking about so far...'

'Out with it,' demands Tasha. 'We can't let this delicious food go to waste.'

'Fame.'

'I should have guessed,' hoots Siobhàn, breaking into gales of laughter.

'What's so funny about that?' Claire wants to know.

'Nothing, petal. It's just so you. You spend all your time reading those upmarket magazines about the rich and beautiful – what else would you be wanting to talk about?'

'I think it could be a good one to bat around,' says John.

'Yeah, but you're a big girl's blouse,' snorts Tasha. 'Can I pour you another camomile tea?'

'Piss off Tasha,' he retorts. 'We can't all have your commonsense approach to character assassination. Some of us are challenged with the impediment of a conscience.'

'Don't you get lonely up there, occupying the moral high ground? You must come down and visit us sometime, just to see what it's like in the real world.'

'Now, now, children,' Quentin intervenes. 'What was it, John, that makes you think we can get some mileage out of fame? Unless of course you want to start us off, Claire? No, I thought not. So, John. We're all ears.'

I'm tough, ambitious and I know exactly what I want. If that makes me a bitch – okay.

Madonna

93

'What's the thing we're all looking for?' John asks rhetorically. 'It's to be noticed, isn't it? We want our lousy existence on this planet to have been of some significance, to have made a difference in some way. And the only way we can know if we've made a difference is if someone else notices us. So life becomes an ongoing quest for fame. If your name appears in any public document, even if it's the court reports in the newspaper, what do you do? You rush down to the newsagent to buy a copy. Why do kids jump up and down and make idiots of themselves behind television reporters on location? Because they're hungry to be *seen*, that's why. We all watch ourselves in shop windows to see how we look, to know how others see us. We want attention.

In the future everybody will be world-famous for fifteen minutes.

Andy Warhol

'The interesting part about it is, that the more we crave attention, the harder it is to get. There's how many billion people on the planet, and most of them jumping up and down in the vain hope that they'll be noticed. Once we lived in small communities: tribes, clans, villages. All you had to do to get noticed was win a baking competition for the church cake-stall or score a goal at the annual picnic's football game. Then we got cities and you needed to be in the paper to make a splash. And now it's television. A moment of fame on TV is massive in its spread, but is thousands of times harder to achieve.

'So we promote the highest ideal in the universe as that of making it onto national TV, but at the same time we make it virtually impossible to

94

attain. So what happens? Ninety-nine per cent of the population lie awake at night wondering why they've lived such insignificant lives, while the other one per cent mop up the entire adulation of society. It's like putting a bowl of water next to a man dying of thirst, but in such a way that he can't reach it. Fame is the hottest industry in town, but it's based on illusion and cruelty. All these kids wanting to be in a famous band, or to be a famous model, or a famous actor. And almost all of them will never make it. What sort of a game is that to be playing?'

'I'm more interested in the people who do get famous,' Claire informs, 'and how they got to be where they are. You're trying to make it into something political, John, but it's not. That's why I like finding out about high-profile people: it's above all that murky side of life.'

'Tell us, Claire,' suggests Quentin, 'what it is you find so fascinating about the rich and famous.'

'Most people become famous because of something within them. You can pretend it's all because of luck or manipulation or something, but I believe it's because they've got some talent or quality which lifts them above the ordinary. I'm interested in them because I think they have something to teach me about reaching my potential.'

'But not all of them, surely?' Quentin puzzles. 'What about Hitler or Charles Manson?'

> **To want fame is to prefer dying scorned than forgotten.**
> E.M. Cioran

> **Celebrity-worship and hero-worship should not be confused. Yet we confuse them every day, and by doing so we come dangerously close to depriving ourselves of all real models. We lose sight of the men and women who do not simply seem great because they are famous, but are famous because they are great. We come closer and closer to degrading all fame into notoriety.**
> Daniel J. Boorstin

'Not awful people, of course. I would have thought they were infamous rather than famous. But even they can teach us about the dark side of humanity, I suppose.'

'But why do you have all those tawdry bits of royal paraphernalia around your room? You're not holding them up as role models, are you?' asks Siobhàn incredulously.

'I don't mind admitting I'm a royalist. Everything gets reduced to its lowest common denominator in this world, and I think we need some people we can look up to, and who can provide some character and gentility to life.'

'Not to mention adultery,' carps Siobhàn.

Christianity will go. It will vanish and shrink. I needn't argue with that; I'm right and I will be proved right. We're more popular than Jesus now; I don't know which will go first — rock and roll or Christianity.

John Lennon

'I remember seeing a documentary about John Lennon,' says Tasha. 'There was a huge argument when he made a passing comment that the Beatles were more famous than Jesus.'

'That's right,' recalls Quentin, 'the funny thing was that they probably were at the time.'

'What great qualities did John Lennon bring to the world, Claire?' Tasha asks.

'I never liked him — I thought he was quite common. But he must have been good at music, mustn't he? Or at least a lot of people thought so.'

'That's like saying Picasso could draw a bit,' grumbles Quentin. 'John Lennon was a philosopher-poet. He was a bloody working-class hero if ever there was one. Listen to "Imagine" — it's one of the great pieces of writing to come out of the twentieth century. But coming back to John's point, it's interesting to compare the Beatles and Jesus. How many people were there in Israel when Jesus died? A few hundred thousand? He might have been famous in his time, but what hope would he have in today's world? Could Jesus get on TV? Not a dog's chance, I wouldn't think, unless he could play guitar. The Beatles would've pushed him off prime time.'

'Exactly,' agrees John. 'And if Jesus can't cut it in the big bad media world, what hope is there for any of us?'

Claire has begun to pout. 'Just because something's hard, that doesn't mean you should give up on it. What are you suggesting, John? That we all accept that our lives are mediocre and insignificant?'

'You're half right. I wouldn't describe anyone's life as mediocre or insignificant, but if fame's your idea of significance then I'd say let's be free of it. It's all bullshit. You don't have to have your face on TV or in the paper to be important. People are important simply because of who they are. By focusing on a few privileged brats who hit the big time, we're consigning millions of good ordinary people to the rubbish heap.'

'But that's where you're wrong,' Claire finds the courage to counter. 'We may not be mediocre, but most of us live as if we were. We settle for too little. It needs people with verve and courage to show us what's possible in life. That's what fame is about — it's the recognition of something

> **John was in constant need of proof of love and security and he was constantly testing people for that proof.**
>
> Cynthia Lennon

> **To become a celebrity is to become a brand name. There is Ivory Soap, Rice Krispies, and Philip Roth. Ivory is the soap that floats; Rice Krispies is the breakfast cereal that goes snap-crackle-pop; Philip Roth is the Jew who masturbates with a piece of liver.**
>
> Philip Roth

special that we want to hold up in front of us so that we don't forget what we're capable of.'

'Like the photo of Dachau I keep in my room,' says John unhelpfully.

'I had an auntie who was almost famous,' muses Tasha.

'Well?' demands Siobhàn. 'Don't tease.'

'She was my father's youngest sister, Emily. The family were all quite musical, apparently, but Emily had a voice to die for. No one had much money, but they decided she should get classical training. She was a soprano. My uncle said she would make him cry every time she sang, and that's no mean feat. Anyway, she kept winning all these competitions, and eventually she was accepted into an Italian programme for the development of young opera singers. When she came back she sang soprano in a production of *Madame Butterfly* and there were rave reviews.'

'Not Emily Durham?' asks Quentin in a sudden flash of revelation. 'Oh god, I know this story,' he adds in response to Tasha's nod.

'She loved being on stage and singing, but it came at a cost. Suddenly everyone wanted to talk to her and celebrate her success. She was fêted by the great patrons of the opera. It was a huge leap in class, of course. Emily grew up in a working-class home, and she had no idea how to behave in high society. She made a few embarrassing gaffes, including getting drunk at a cocktail evening and vomiting into an umbrella stand. She didn't really belong there, but she didn't fit at home anymore either.

'Uncle John says she would arrive back in Islington throwing money all around the place, and trying to show how sophisticated she was by refusing to eat home-cooked meals. Her parents were awfully proud of her, but they didn't like what she had become. They were basic but decent folk, and when she announced one night that she was going out to "fuck a Frenchman", there was a terrific row. Her father told her to leave and come back when she'd found a civil tongue. Emily vowed that she wouldn't darken the door for quids.

'Meanwhile her career was booming. There were some ridiculous comparisons made of her, and they were already starting to throw around the word "diva" when she was only twenty-six. She was in magazines and newspapers all over the place – I've got a few articles stashed away somewhere. But her behaviour was becoming increasingly bizarre. She'd stay up all night, ringing people with wild plans and schemes. My father went to visit her at her hotel, and she insisted that they fly to Paris for a coffee. She had a performance the following night, but off they went and got back again in time for her to sing. Dad put it down to artistic temperament, apparently.

'And then she crashed. The manager of the opera company gets a phone call in the middle of the night, and is called up to her hotel room.

I'm afraid of losing my obscurity. Genuineness only thrives in the dark. Like celery.

Aldous Huxley

It is dangerous to let the public behind the scenes. They are easily disillusioned and then they are angry with you, for it was the illusion they loved.

W. Somerset Maugham

There's blood from one end of the bathroom to the other. She's attempted to slash her wrists. They rush her off to hospital and she survives, but she's in deep depression. The doctors bring in a psychiatrist, and it's discovered that she's bipolar – what they used to call manic-depressive. The medication is quite good, and promises her an almost normal life. But it's the end of the career, bang – just like that. They dropped her so fast that you couldn't see it happen. No one wanted to know her. She disappeared off the public stage.

'She married someone she'd met in hospital, a taxi-driver. They settled down in a semi-detached in South London, with a couple of cats. My only memory of her is going to visit them once with my parents when I was about six. Emily was beautiful, but a bit vague, I thought. A year or so later she was killed in a car accident – hit a pole. The family always wondered afterwards if it had been suicide, but there was no evidence. So that was Emily.'

'Did she ever sing again, after she was diagnosed?' asks Claire.

'No, at least as far as I know, never. Unless it was in the shower.'

'Okay, quick quiz,' suggests John. 'How many of us here want to be famous?'

'Hell, no,' Siobhàn insists. 'I'm happy enough doing my thing off in a corner. I hope some people may appreciate my work, but as long as I'm pleased with it and I keep getting paid, it's all

> A legend is an old man with a cane known for what he used to do. I'm still doing it.
>
> Miles Davis

right with me. My great quest for world domination ended at age eighteen, when my art teacher asked me if I'd ever considered architectural drafting.'

'I don't know about fame,' Quentin ponders. 'I'd like to get published and have people read my writing. The more that read it the better, I suppose. But that's got nothing to do with earning lots of money or being recognized in the street or anything. Writing's like a conversation with the world, and if no one's listening then you're talking to yourself. So yeah, I want to be known, but only so that people will read me.'

'I don't like to say,' says Claire. 'You're all so modest — it makes me sound terribly ambitious, which I'm not. But I'd love to be famous. I want people to know me wherever I go, and have to take holidays in secret so that I can get some peace. I'd like to see my name in the papers and my face on the screen. And to have so much money that I didn't have to think about it ever again. I could stand a little adulation.'

'Doing what?' asks Tasha, incredulous.

'I don't know,' admits Claire. Her face crumples.

'I think it's all a load of bollocks,' Tasha continues. 'For me it's enough to be a household name in my own household. I don't give a shit whether I get noticed or not. I've got work to do that I'm happy doing, and there's enough excitement just living without having to do it in front of crowds.'

'And what about the quizmaster?' Siobhàn asks.

True glory consists in doing what deserves to be written; in writing what deserves to be read; and in so living as to make the world happier and better for our living in it.
Pliny the Elder

'No, it holds no appeal for me at all,' explains John. 'But I have to admit I'd like to contribute something significant to the world on the way through.'

'Isn't that the same thing?' Claire inquires.

'Not at all. You can do good and important things which don't attract much attention, but are still significant.'

'Yeah? Like what?' Siobhàn wants to know.

'Our next door neighbour was a widow. Her husband had died of a heart attack, and she brought up her three kids on her own. Just after the last one left home, her mother got sick, with Parkinson's Disease. So she takes her mother in, and looks after her for the next eight years until she dies. No big song and dance about it – just quiet, loving care. She was a bloody hero, in my book.'

'But if a tree falls in a forest, does it make a noise?' asks Quentin.

'What on earth are you talking about?' a very puzzled Claire wonders.

'He's saying it's not significant if no one knows about it,' John interprets. 'But that's just an indication of how sick our society has got.'

'Thanks very much,' Quentin grins.

'There have got to be some things that are good in themselves, haven't there? Irrespective of whether anyone knows about them or not. If we're just performing for an audience, then we'll do whatever keeps the punters happy. Which is not a bad description for what we've got at the moment, in my humble opinion.'

'I think you were right earlier on when you talked about wanting to be noticed,' Quentin argues. 'Is there anything wrong with that? We're drowning in this sea of protoplasm out here, sinking without trace amongst the muffled millions. All of us just want to put our hands up and say, "Hey, look here. I've got something to offer." We want to be special, it's a human thing.'

'Yes,' adds Claire, 'that's it exactly. I want to be special.'

'But don't you see that you *are* special?' John retorts. 'If you don't believe that, it doesn't matter how many people tell you that you are – you won't accept it. Look at Marilyn Monroe or Kurt Cobain. They died of fame, because underneath all the hype, they felt like shit. If you know that you already are special, then you can just get on with the business of being yourself, because there's nothing else to prove.'

'That's all very well,' chimes in Quentin. 'But I want to leave something behind. I don't want my passage through life to be forgotten.'

'I remember being on holiday at a place up in the north of New Zealand,' John recalls. 'I went walking with a friend of mine along the beach. We talked about all sorts of things, as you do. It was the new year, and so we were thinking about where

Within the limits of her biology and intellect, Monroe went as far as it is possible for a human to travel into the hyperspace of fame. After this occurred, sex, high culture, temptations and the sating of earthly desires had lost all attractive charms for her. She had realized the limits of how far the body can take one.

Douglas Coupland

we'd got to in life – that sort of thing. We decided to write down lists of what we hoped to achieve in the next year. So we each got a stick, and wrote these words in the sand, and then stood back and looked at them. It felt really good. But the next day, I got up early and went back to the same beach. The words were all gone. The tide had come in and washed them all away. It taught me something important.'

'Which is?' asks Quentin.

'That if you're going to leave something behind, you need to be careful where you leave it.'

'Why is it that we want to be remembered, anyway?' Tasha wonders. 'Just living and enjoying it should be enough, surely.'

'It's the big M word, isn't it?' Quentin decides. 'We want meaning with our existence. No matter how much we argue there isn't any, we're still hungry for it at the end of the day.'

'Continuity, I'd say,' Siobhàn contributes. 'It used to be through families. Everyone would have as many kids as they could so that some would survive and carry forward the family name. Then you got to be part of the genealogy, and it meant your story carried on after you'd died. Now we don't want any ankle-biters 'cause they get in the way of our *lifestyles*. So we need someone else to do the remembering for us. Maybe the general public can be our family. Maybe we can get our name in the news.'

'I guess once eternal life in heaven's been

Fame is no sanctuary from the passing of youth... suicide is much easier and more acceptable in Hollywood than growing old gracefully.

Julie Burchill

deconstructed, memory is the only place left to settle down and have a good death,' agrees John.

'It's a sickness,' Tasha objects. 'Bloody male egotism if you ask me. History is the story of men. Who knows the name of all the women who lived and died and made a difference? They just got on with it and did it, without anyone to take notes or photos. It's a male erection thing, I'm sure of it. Look at these mad bastards shooting someone famous so that *they* can be famous for doing it. All men; all worried that their life has gone flaccid.'

'I continue to hope for the res-erection,' says Quentin.

'Long may it last,' adds Siobhàn.

'I had thought we were fairly safe with fame for a topic,' Claire complains. 'Anyone for more?'

Neither fame nor money add storyline to one's life. This is, since biblical times, the irony of human pursuit...

Douglas Coupland

Chapter Six

'Do you smoke, man?'

'Yeah, I do,' John admits.

'Nah, I mean smoke as in *smoke*, man,' his client explains, extracting a honey-brown block from a matchbox. He winks at John.

They are sitting at the kitchen table in a basement flat. Mould has blackened the walls. The air is so heavy with damp that words flatten against it. A gas cooker is buried under a collection of metal, which may possibly be related to the preparation of food. Alongside it, the bench is concealed under plates, takeaway containers, ashtrays and scraps of food in various stages of putrefaction. For some minutes John has been trying to ignore the activity of a mouse which nibbles sedately in a corner, oblivious to human presence.

'I don't think that's a good idea,' responds John mildly. 'I need to get some information off you before we can process your application.'

'I need to get high, man, that's what I need,' Rupert Simpson, unemployed printer's assistant of Hackney, explains. He continues construction of a paper chillum with all the care of a craftsman.

A child with a grey T-shirt and no knickers wanders into the room. She looks about three years old, and John notices the open sore on her neck, and the bruises on her arm. Her eyes have

I hate to advocate drugs, alcohol, violence or insanity to anyone, but they've always worked for me.

Hunter S. Thompson

the bored vacancy which John has come to associate with his work. In her hand she has a small foil packet. It's a condom. She sidles up to her father, chewing on the edge of her treasure, and watching what he is doing.

'Piss off, Tanya,' he says without looking at her. 'Go and watch the telly.' She ambles off back out the door. Meanwhile Rupert is sucking hard on his newly finished masterpiece. He finally opens his eyes and exhales, sighing in approximation of religious ecstasy.

'How long since your partner left you?' asks John, turning his attention back to the form on the clipboard.

The poverty of the poor is their ruin.
The Bible

Claire fishes in her bag to find the letter. Anything to distract her from the crush of bodies on the tube. It is perhaps the third time she has read it, and she is picking up fresh nuances with every examination.

Dearest Claire,

Lovely to hear from you as always. Thank you for remembering our anniversary, and of course the clock was just beautiful. I have placed it on the mantelpiece in the drawing room, and shall think of you whenever I look at it. You shouldn't have gone to such trouble and expense – there was no need, although of course it was a rather special occasion for us.

We planned to go out for dinner to celebrate, but unfortunately Daddy was unable to get back from Bristol that night, and we had to postpone it until the following evening. I was a little disappointed, but that's part of accepting the demands of your father's work. I'm afraid I may have overreacted a little when he returned, with the consequence that our anniversary dinner was a little strained.

Have you managed to change your job yet? I do hope so. You have so much unfulfilled potential, and it saddens us to see it go to waste. Please don't take this as a criticism, dear – we want only what will make you happy. But we also know what you're capable of, and I don't think you're achieving it at present. I'm not one to talk, of course, but your father had such high hopes for you.

I'm afraid I have to tell you that Miriam is not very well. I received a letter from the hospital to say she had been readmitted. Apparently she had stopped taking her medication once again, and the police had taken her into custody after she began removing her clothing at Sainsbury's. It's all so terribly tragic and embarrassing. I went down to see her last Sunday. Daddy won't come any more as it distresses him too much. I must say that I find it awfully upsetting myself. I can't bear all the locked doors, and the nurses carrying rings of keys as if they were jailers.

Miriam was heavily medicated, and not capable of any meaningful conversation. I imagine she was pleased to see me, though there was little indication of it. She looks dreadful. She has put on a great deal of weight, and her hair is completely uncared for. I do wish the hospital would encourage a little more attention to grooming and hygiene. The nurse was not very receptive to my comments in this regard. Do pray for your sister, darling. I don't know what else there is to be done.

I have been kept busy with the Women's Guild, and my

Sometimes accidents happen in life from which we have need of a little madness to extricate ourselves successfully.

La Rochefoucauld

name has been put forward to be secretary next year.
I'm not sure that I really want all the extra responsibility,
though I will be happy to serve if that is the wish of the
members. Your father is as ever, and continues to work
harder than he should. His patience seems to be wearing
thinner as he gets older, but I imagine this is to be
expected.

I do worry about you, Claire. I wish you would find
decent digs on your own somewhere, instead of flatting
with strangers. I'm probably old-fashioned, but the
potential for catastrophe looms large in my imagination.
Please be careful.

Love, Mummy

There's that moment of opening your eyes and
not recognizing the ceiling. Siobhàn struggles to
put the pieces together. There are various images
swimming in her visual field, but thus far they
have not combined to any effect. A poster of Tina
Turner is watching over her. A man's leg is resting
heavily in her groin. She has a strand of her own
hair stuck in her mouth. The air contains the
mustiness of sweat, sex and stale alcohol which
has become so familiar. Light is strengthening
through a pale yellow curtain which has seen
better days. The bed beneath her back is softer
than her own. That may account for her sore back,
but she suspects not.

She glances across to the back of the man's
head, which is buried in a pillow. The blond hair
stirs memory. Rex. The assistant copy-editor with
the huge ego. The drinks after work. Bits of it

Like the bee its sting,
the promiscuous leave
behind them in each
encounter something
of themselves by
which they are made
to suffer.

Cyril Connolly

surface into consciousness, none of them welcome. She closes her eyes, hoping against hope that something will have changed when they open again. Soon her breathing has become deep and regular.

Quentin finds Claire tucked up into an armchair, sucking her thumb and staring out of the window.

'The beautiful Claire,' he sighs. 'You know I love you.'

'Don't be silly, Quentin. I'm not in the mood for it.'

'Ah, my sad-eyed queen, what is it? Tell Uncle Quentin all your troubles.' He kneels beside the chair and takes her hand, stroking it.

'Do you have secrets?' she asks. 'Things you can't bear to talk about?'

'My dear, secrets are my treasury. Writers feed off the fermentation of great lumps of concealed misery submerged in their psyches. Take away my secrets and I would be barren.'

'Why is life so beastly sometimes?'

'I seem to have temporarily misplaced my devastating analysis of the problem of suffering in human existence. But in the meantime, I'm happy to listen if you want to talk. You're so fragile, Claire. Nothing beastly should happen to you.' And he kisses her hand gently.

'I don't know. I've never talked about this to anyone outside my family. But sometimes I think it's just too much to keep it all hushed up. I'm not

> I not only have my secrets, I am my secrets. And you are your secrets. Our secrets are human secrets, and our trusting each other enough to share them with each other has much to do with the secret of what it is to be human.
>
> Frederick Buechner

strong enough to carry it on my own. But then I don't want to talk about it either. And Mummy would be furious if she thought I was parading family secrets.'

There is a long period of silence. Quentin follows his instincts and refrains from comment.

'I have a sister,' she says eventually. 'A younger sister, Miriam. We were quite close, growing up. Totally different personalities. She was wild and carefree and fun, and I was the serious one who worried about consequences. Perhaps it was because we were so different that we got on so well. She was always moody, but when she was happy she made everyone laugh, even Daddy. Miriam was very bright − she could have done much better than me at school, except that she lived for her social life.

'It was the year after her fifteenth birthday that things started to go wrong. She made some bizarre comments to me, and I began to suspect that she was experimenting with drugs. She kept talking about this enormously complex conspiracy, in which parking wardens were secretly Nazis, employed by the state to keep surveillance on us all. Apparently they were following her and making notes about her activity. They pretended to be issuing tickets, but really they were making reports back to their masters.

'I tried to keep an open mind, but I became more and more concerned. I talked to my mother about it, but she said it was probably just an adolescent stage and not to worry. Then I came home one day and there was a police car outside the house. Miriam had attacked a parking warden with a hockey stick. They took her into custody, but soon realized that she needed a medical examination. She was diagnosed as a paranoid schizophrenic, and admitted to hospital.

'That was the beginning of it all. I must have been naïve; I think we all were. I expected that the doctors would be able to make her well again. I really did believe that it was something temporary, and that soon she'd be back to her old self. When she came out of hospital she was on pills. They made her better apparently, though it was hard to see how. It was as if something inside her had died. She was still Miriam, but a much slower and tamer version of herself. I hated it; I was scared of her. When she said she was feeling better and didn't need to take the pills anymore, I was happy.

'For a few days it seemed as if she was back to normal again. But then it started all over again. Hearing secret messages being broadcast on the radio. Getting direct commands from God. It wasn't long until she smashed up everything in her room, and was back in hospital again. Psychiatric illness is a life sentence; that's what I found out. She'll never ever get better. The pills help her to be able to live without causing a fuss, but they smother her and so she throws them away and gets sick again. It's a never-ending cycle. I feel as if she's been kidnapped, except that she's still here.

'Sometimes I hate her, Quentin. Isn't that

112

terrible? I want to shake her and tell her to stop being so stupid; to stop causing us so much pain. And then other times I'm so sad for her, and then I want to hold her and cuddle her and protect her. My parents can't talk about it without fighting. My father blames it on my mother's side of the family, and Mummy simply cries. There's no one to fight or blame or attack. That's the worst part of it – it's nobody's fault, so you're supposed to just accept it. But sometimes I can't, and I don't know what to do about it.'

Quentin holds her hand against his face, caressing it.

'What brought all this on?' he asks after some time.

'It was Tasha, talking about her auntie. I wanted to say something then, but I wasn't brave enough. You won't tell anyone, will you, Quentin? I know it's silly, but I simply couldn't bear it if other people knew. I shouldn't have told you, really.'

'You can trust me. Though I have to say that the only thing I've learned about my own secrets is that they breed in darkness. Anytime you want to talk about Miriam, or just have a good old weep on my shoulder, I'll be around, darling. But look at you! Your make-up is ruined, you old hag!'

Claire manages a smile beneath the weight.

There's not enough bloody light at the door, that's the trouble. John fumbles with his key and drops it to the ground. It bounces away into hiding. He spends some time on his hands and

You want to hear about insanity? I was found running naked through the jungles in Mexico. At the Mexico City airport, I decided I was in the middle of a movie and walked out on the wing on takeoff. My body... my liver... okay, my brain... went.

Dennis Hopper

knees in fruitless searching. Standing up too quickly, he staggers slightly and realizes he may have had more to drink than he meant to.

'Shit!' he proclaims, pressing his forehead against the door. It's late; too late really. John eyes the climb to his bedroom window, before dismissing it. He concedes defeat and knocks on the door.

Nothing happens. He fumbles about on the ground again, coming up empty-handed. He's about to knock again when the door opens, and he stumbles in astonishment. Tasha is standing there in a dressing gown and lime-green fluffy slippers. She doesn't look very friendly.

'Tasha, you're a bloody angel, you are. An angel in slippers,' he qualifies. 'My key,' he adds in response to the silence. 'I lost it.'

'You're drunk,' she accuses.

'Has anyone ever told you,' mumbles John, 'how fetching you look in that dressing-gown?'

'Get inside. It's cold with the door open, and I've got better things to be doing than talking to pissed flatmates at two in the morning,' she growls.

John makes exaggerated tiptoeing movements through the doorway, which throws him off balance. He reaches out for the wall, but his hand falls instead on the wall-mounted telephone. It rips off its mounting under his weight, and both John and the telephone fall to the floor.

'You stupid fucking bastard!' responds Tasha in a hoarse whisper. 'Get up!'

Drink! for you know not whence you came, nor why: Drink! for you know not why you go, nor where.

Omar Khayyam

114

John shakes his head slowly and stumbles to his feet. 'Sorry, Tasha, sorry.'

'You're a sorry bastard, all right. If you're going to carry on like this, maybe you should find somewhere else to live.'

'I'm sorry, I'm sorry. But Tasha?'

'What?'

'Give us a kiss.'

She lifts her knee between his legs and leaves him groaning and laughing. She can't remember the last time she felt this angry.

Siobhàn jumps the queue and starts the next cycle, but she cheats.

'What's this?' Quentin demands.

'Ah, what's it bloody well look like then? Sure and you've seen pizza before in your godforsaken life.'

'I know what it is; I just don't know what it represents. You're supposed to be cooking, not ordering in pizza.'

'Well I couldn't be stuffed, so to speak. So I thought to myself, it's the talking that's important, and we can do that as well over pizza as filet mignon. Besides, I've ordered four different types and there's plenty of wine to wash it down with. Now, does anyone want to argue with me?'

'I never said a word,' says Quentin.

'And our topic for tonight is?' inquires John around a clinging strand of mozzarella.

'Family,' Siobhàn states, daring opposition.

'I'm glad you didn't cook anything then,' John grins, 'seeing I'll be losing my appetite.'

'Scary stuff,' Quentin agrees. 'I think families are the real scourge of the earth. Forget AIDS and Ebola — someone'll find a vaccine for them one day. But there's no protection against family.'

'Let's be fair,' Siobhàn pleads. 'Did anyone have a happy childhood, apart from myself?'

'Mine wasn't too bad, in comparison,' says John thoughtfully.

'Didn't seem to do much for you,' sneers Tasha.

'Oooh, talons away, Tasha; no blood until dessert. That's if we're having dessert?' Quentin pleads.

'Wait and see,' is all that Siobhàn will say. 'Now tell us what was good about your family, John.'

'It was a rough ride at times. I was third of six — an older brother and sister, and three younger sisters. We'd fight all the time of course, unless we were fighting someone else and then we'd all look out for each other. My parents loved us and we had a lot of fun together, especially on holiday. We always had terrific rows around the table, but usually good-natured. I got some bruises on the way through, but mostly I look back on childhood as a good time.'

'What universe are you from? You must be the sole survivor of Happy Planet,' mocks Tasha.

'What do you want me to do, invent a miserable family to reinforce your stereotypes?' retorts John. 'God knows I see enough dysfunctional families in my work to have no illusions.'

'Being a know-all social worker visiting "dysfunctional families" and writing reports is not quite the same as growing up in one, if you'll excuse my cynicism,' continues Tasha. 'My family is what I've had to overcome in order to live. It's my burden, my living nightmare, my own personal emotional cancer. The only way to survive was to resist. I fostered my hatred of my mother, because I knew it was the only means I had of staying outside her web.'

'You have to admit your childhood was unusual,' Claire objects. 'You can't generalize on the basis of that experience.'

'That's where you're wrong,' Tasha insists. 'You think I'm unusual because my father upped and died on me, and my mother was alcoholic? Bollocks. That's the pattern, the norm, the everyday home-and-garden reality. Not the details of course, but the effect – the suffering, the emotional and psychological baggage, the outright humiliation. As far as I'm concerned, family is the greatest social evil ever invented.'

'Sounding a trifle victim-like?' riles John.

'Don't you pull my chain, you kiwi prick! I'm not looking for sympathy – I'm telling you that happy families are a fairy-tale, that's all. The sooner we all wake up and smell the coffee and take responsibility for ourselves the better. I'm glad that my family was so obviously screwed because it taught me what the world is like and how to fight. People like you are still treating the world like your mother's tit, wanting to suck on it and feel warm and safe.'

Families are about love overcoming emotional torture.
Matt Groening

·········

'It's a weird thing,' says Quentin, 'what happens when I get together with my family. We're okay as long as we're apart. But put us all together at Christmas or a family wedding and all hell breaks loose.'

'Strange but true,' agrees Siobhàn. 'As soon as I get within a fifty-mile radius of my folks, I revert to patterns of reacting that I thought were long gone. Somehow all my buttons get pushed and the worst of me comes out.'

'It's because everyone knows you as you were,' Claire ventures. 'Their understanding stops at the point at which you left home and started to become independent. So they want you back as you were, and that person doesn't exist any more.'

There is a moment of quiet as the others stare at Claire in astonishment. She simply sweeps the hair back off her face and smiles. 'What?' she says.

'I remember going home for my parents' silver wedding,' Quentin muses. 'It was in the summer and they'd put up a big marquee out the back for a celebration party. I was twenty-two, and I'd just got back from a couple of weeks in Paris, staying with an artist friend of mine. I knew things were going to be bad when my mother scowled at the clothes I was wearing, and suggested I borrow something of Dad's. Then my sister Katie arrived, and I could see straight away that she was upset and trying to put a brave face on things.

'I managed to get a few minutes with her alone,

and tried to find out what was wrong. She'd just broken up with her partner, after being together for a couple of years. And then she found she was pregnant. So she had an abortion. All very staunch and matter-of-fact about it until it was over, and then she fell apart. This had all been just a week before, and now she had to try to survive the gathering of the clan and so on. She made me swear not to let on to our parents.

'Of course my mother has some sort of emotional sonar which seeks out trouble at any depth. She knew there was something up, but Katie denied it and took refuge in the busyness of getting ready. The people arrived — all the aunts and uncles and cousins that we did our best to ignore in any given year. It was so predictable and awful. Pot-bellied middle-aged men eyeing up the twenty-year-olds in short dresses, and making sure they had a 'family' kiss. Their wives drinking too much champagne and shrieking like tarts. And then the speeches. So godawful dull and lifeless. Made you want to top yourself or piss in the punch or something.

'I was keeping an eye on Katie, and could see disaster approaching with each glass she threw back. Before long she was absolutely pie-eyed and maudlin. She started weeping none too quietly, and Mum rescued her from the very physical comfort of one of the uncles. It all came out then. My mother was howling over the loss of her first grandchild, and that attracted the attention of my father. Once he pieced together what was going on

When you deal with your brother, be pleasant, but get a witness.
Hesiod

he started in on Katie, calling her a stupid bitch and so on. I was in the middle, terrified that any minute there was going to be physical violence.

'Here we were supposed to be toasting twenty-five years of wedded familial bliss, and there's enough emotional cruelty going down to keep the Freudians employed for decades. The whole family unit is either crying or shouting, my father's calling me a useless poof and Katie a slut, and there's a crowd of uncles looking on, wondering when it's time to start punching someone. It was magic! I vowed then and there that I would manufacture a supply of excuses for why I couldn't attend future family functions.'

'I want to hear some more of Tasha's story,' requests Siobhàn. She has been quietly noting Tasha's body language.

'It's not something I like to talk about,' Tasha ducks.

'Tell us how you survived,' Siobhàn insists.

'I got very old very quickly. I became a mother to the boys, because they didn't have one. She was another child – worse than the others, because she thought she was in charge. Everything I tried to put in place to help us get by, she tried to destroy. She hated me taking over – it rubbed her face in the fact that she was a failure. And then there would be the periods of remorse, which were the worst of all. She had to confess and repent and try and make amends. She disgusted me. It only ever lasted a day or two, and she'd be back on the bottle again.

The most socially subversive institution of our time is the one-parent family.

Paul Johnson

'I found an old photo of her — she must have been about eighteen, I suppose, and incredibly beautiful. I put it in my room, and I would take it out and look at it. This lovely woman had been my mother, I decided, but she had died. The ugly hag who inhabited the house and made our lives miserable was a fraud, and we had to survive in spite of her. My mother was my enemy, and I had to fight against her every step of the way for the sake of the boys. I was the only hope they had, and I was determined that the old witch wasn't going to screw them up.

'She almost beat me. Her bloody genes were the one thing I hadn't counted on. When my brother Robbie started drinking heavily, I started to see all the patterns again, and it was like her revenge on me. But even then I refused to let her win. I fought for him. I hassled the shit out of him, dragged him along to AA meetings, took his money off him and gave him an allowance. And it looks like he's through the worst of it. I tell him if he drinks again, I'll kill him to get it over with quickly.

'But I had to fight every minute of the day; to be strong even when I wanted to cry or run away and hide. I've got no time for namby-pamby liberal bullshit, and "at-risk" families. It's a whole bloody industry, and doesn't change squat. Some people don't deserve to have kids because they haven't learned how to look after themselves. You need a licence to drive a car, for god's sake, but any dipshit with a hole between her legs is entitled to

Once we truly know that life is difficult — once we truly understand and accept it — then life is no longer difficult. Because once it is accepted, it no longer matters.
M. Scott Peck

have a baby. And pass on the crap from generation to generation.'

'I think I need a drink,' says Quentin.

'What's the alternative?' asks John.

'How do you mean?' Siobhàn inquires.

'If families are so awful, and I don't need any convincing that they are, what are the other options? You still need a couple of people to at least start the ball rolling in procreation. Do we call it quits as a human race and outlaw pregnancy? Maybe we could produce babies outside of a womb, sort of *Brave New World* stuff. But then who brings them up? Would it be any better if the community took over?'

'Save us,' Tasha cries. 'That's the essence of communism, isn't it? The state knows best. Give us your children and we'll make them into good little comrades. Of course there's no alternative to families, and just because I had a shitty childhood doesn't mean that there's no hope for anyone in the future. But we've got to make some changes, and the first step is getting rid of this rosy picture of family life as some warm fuzzy thing that happens whenever two people get together and start bonking.'

'I still want kids,' Siobhàn throws in, puzzled at herself.

'Well you're getting plenty of practice at the mechanics,' says Quentin. Siobhàn lunges at him with a knife, and he ducks beneath the table.

'It's a primal thing, isn't it?' she continues. 'You always think that you can do better than your

> Call it a clan, call it a network, call it a family: whatever you call it, whoever you are, you need one.
>
> Jane Howard

parents did. Even when you convince yourself that you don't want babies, you walk past a pram in the street and your hormones jump out and ambush you. It's useless to resist. I mean, why would any woman go through with that much pain if there was any logic in it? It's a programming thing.'

'Bullshit!' retorts Tasha. 'We've all got choices and we're responsible for them. If you choose to have kids, then damn well own up to the fact that it's a decision you've made, and do what you can to prepare yourself for it. The days of genetic determinism are behind us, sister. You don't have to do anything you don't want to.'

> The family you come from isn't as important as the family you're going to have.
>
> Ring Lardner

'It's strange the way the myth keeps going. I would have thought it would have been splintered on the rocks of reality by now,' Quentin frowns. 'And yet we still play happy families as if it's a possibility, let alone a likelihood.'

'It's sponsored by the wedding industry,' jokes Siobhàn. 'What would they be doing with all that white satin and velvet if there were no suckers to keep on believing? I can hardly bear to go to a wedding now. It's like the commissioning of the *Titanic* all over again. I feel like shouting out in the middle of it all.'

'You don't have to write off the entire possibility of marriage, just because a lot of them are failing,' Claire objects.

'Darling, that's my thought exactly,' quips Quentin. 'When you marry me you'll be the most divine bride of the whole century.'

'In your dreams, Quentin. You're all being too negative, as usual. Siobhàn here wants children, and so do I, given the right circumstances. And when I do, I want them to grow up in a stable environment with both male and female role models. I hope that I can help to build a family where there's security and love.'

'Hope is one thing,' objects Tasha. 'Reality is something different altogether. Why do you assume that you're different from everyone else? That's what it means, statistically speaking. If you look at the figures, what you're saying is that you're going to beat the odds. Well, gambling's okay if that's what you're into, but not with other people's lives.'

'So you're a better person by not taking the risk?' Claire demands. 'You keep yourself pure by playing safe? I think that's ultimately selfish. Of course it's dangerous, of course things can go wrong. But look at all of us. Whatever mistakes our parents may have made, we're here because they took a chance. And even with your dreadful mother, Tasha, surely you don't want to say that life hasn't been worth it, that you wish you'd never been born? Life is messy and horrible, but I think we need to be involved!'

'That's one up to Claire, I'd say,' John referees.

'And this, as they say, is to finish with,' declares Siobhàn. She places a dish in the centre of the table with a flourish.

'It's not...' begins John.

124

'Bread-and-butter pudding; yes, it is,' Siobhàn confirms. 'With a whisky sauce that my grandmother taught me. This is the best of Irish haute cuisine.'

'Ah, takes me back to my childhood,' enthuses John. 'Bread-and-butter pudding with lashings of fresh cream — my favourite favourite.'

'We used to get it at school,' Claire says distastefully. 'I think I might pass.'

'My arse you'll pass. This is fruit of the family kitchen, and there'll be no resistance brooked. Try it and see — I'll be surprised if it tastes anything like what you had at school.'

> A home without a grandmother is like an egg without salt.
>
> Florence King

'You know the other night when I came home drunk,' says John to Tasha afterwards. 'I'm sorry about that. I have some idea why you were so pissed off with me.'

'I'm not sure that you do, actually. But okay, thanks. You can buy me chocolate to repent.'

Chapter Seven

There's an orgy of cleaning under way. Tasha is cracking the whip, snapping out commands to anyone approaching visible idleness. John's whistling is oddly distorted as his head enters the oven. Siobhàn has a pair of lime-green FM headphones welded to her skull, and makes alarming movements with the vacuum cleaner nozzle as she dances to private rhythms. Quentin is wearing purple rubber gloves and sunglasses with bright yellow frames. He flicks a feather duster with exaggerated gestures. Claire, despite protests regarding her task's irrelevance, is polishing the cutlery.

'Have you done the bookcase?' Tasha interrogates Quentin as he stands back to admire his work.

'Darling, my feathery fingers have caressed every recess. The only thing left to dust is your bust.'

'Get off, you prat,' she growls, retreating and smiling as Quentin stalks her with the duster. 'How about putting the kettle on?'

John watches the way the sunlight shines on an apple in the fruit bowl. It seems to address most of the mysteries of the universe. Around him the conversation loops and weaves. He is silent. Saturday morning is the most human day in the

The graveyards are full of women whose houses were so spotless you could eat off the floor.
Heloise Cruse

week. Full of hope and possibility. How brief is joy.

'God, I loathe work,' declares Quentin.

'How would you *know*?' asks Tasha.

'I love you too. But surely no one can get excited about dusting or cleaning or digging holes in roads or whatever. It's just so mundane and degrading. There's got to be more to life than rubber gloves and oven cleaner.'

'Bloody snob that you are,' quips Siobhàn. 'You wouldn't be spending so much time with your nose in your fooking books if it weren't for the people carting the rubbish away and digging holes to fix the water main. You're a kept man, Quentin, that you are.'

'But just because something has to be done,' he insists, 'doesn't mean that anyone has to pretend to like doing it. I detest cleaning, but I still do it. In my humble opinion, such as it is, too many people get seduced into making the maintenance of life their whole career. A clean oven is a means to the end of a fine meal – it's not an achievement in itself.'

'Hang on,' joins John, stirred from reverie by all the talk of ovens, 'I don't think I can go along with seeing physical work as just a means to some other end. Otherwise it totally devalues work. If it's mainly functional, then most of us spend a fair bit of our lives wasting our time for the sake of something else. I think work has value and meaning in itself, not just for what it achieves.'

> Keep quiet. Do your work in the world, but inwardly keep quiet. Then all will come to you.
>
> Nisaragada Ha Maharaj

There is always the
danger that we may
just do the work for
the sake of the work.
This is where the
respect and the love
and the devotion
come in – that we do
it to God, to Christ,
and that's why we try
to do it as beautifully
as possible.

Mother Teresa

'Listen to yourself,' Quentin retorts. 'You sound like a walking compendium of Chairman Mao. The only reason you can afford to have a high view of work is because you never had to do a shite job. Try standing on the belt in a process factory, or leaning on a jackhammer all day. Then you can come home and tell me about the dignity of work. Most people put up with that sort of crap work because they earn money and can go out and spend it doing what they want to do. The "noble labourer" is a myth to make the rich feel better.'

'For what it's worth, I've worked both in factories and on a road gang. And it was good hard physical work, and at the end of the day I could see what I'd done. In some ways it was a bloody sight better than what I'm doing now. At least I knew I was producing something. And the people I worked with – they were good people. They took a pride in their work, the best of them. You can't look down from the exalted heights of being an artist and write off their labour as being of no value.'

Every job has
drudgery, whether
it is in the home, in
the school, or in the
office. The first secret
of happiness is the
recognition of this
fundamental fact.

M.C. McIntosh

'I'm not writing off either them or their work. I've got a higher view of their value than you seem to have. You're saying that's all they're good for – I'm saying the system is screwed so that they have no choice other than to do crap work. But that given other possibilities, all of them are capable of much more, and would be happier doing it. I believe we're all artists.'

'God help us,' moans Tasha. 'Who'd do the washing up?'

'These muffins are lovely,' says Claire. 'We should go back to that bakery next time. Those Lebanese girls have such wonderful skin.'

'So why are we doing what we're doing?' Siobhàn asks.

'As in drinking cups of tea?' suggests John.

'As in doing the work we're doing. How many of us, if we had a totally blank slate, would be in the jobs we are now? I'm a graphic designer by accident as much as anything. It's all right; it pays the bills, and now and again I enjoy a project I'm working on. But it doesn't fill me with passion or vision. A job is a job is a job.'

'So where do you get a blank slate from?' inquires Tasha. 'There weren't any being handed out when I was growing up. I would have got one if there were a chance. I like the work I do. I don't expect to change the world with it, but I'm good at it, it gives me satisfaction and it pays the bills. One day I might go out on my own, but only after I've built enough of a base to work on. The trouble with you lot, if you want my opinion, is that you expect the world to be a stage on which you can strut your talents and get a round of applause for.'

'I wasn't aware that "us lot" had troubles,' breaks in Quentin, 'though thanks for the analysis. But come on, let's face it. Metaphysics aside, we've all of us only got one shot at the big apple, and then it's a long time in the ground. So why waste it doing stuff we don't want to do?

If your work is becoming uninteresting, so are you. Work is an inanimate thing and can be made lively and interesting only by injecting yourself into it. Your job is only as big as you are.
George C. Hubbs

Why be working for the man when there's dreams bursting to get out?'

'Because that's what life's about!' Tasha declares a little more forcefully than she had anticipated. 'It's hard lines and struggle and pain. There's no fairy godmothers to wave their wands anymore.'

'They all became dykes and found other uses for their wands,' Siobhàn suggests.

'That's not true,' states Claire.

'Listen,' continues Tasha, 'how many people are living out their dreams? Maybe two per cent of the population. And most of them are doing it because they're either incredibly lucky or outrageously rich. The other ninety-eight per cent of us have got a choice. Either we can knuckle down and make the best of the circumstances we've got, or we can lie around pining and moaning because life didn't turn out the way we wanted it to.'

'I'm for pining and moaning,' says Quentin.

'That,' offers Tasha, 'is self-evident.'

'Perhaps,' muses John, 'the reason that ninety-eight per cent of us are just mucking along is because we're too scared to do anything else.'

'What do you mean?' asks Claire.

'Maybe it's just an imagination deficit, or a lack of courage. We don't believe we have the right or the talent to be doing what we want to do, so we settle for something less that pays better.'

'Save us! A world full of starving artists,' predicts Tasha.

'At least artists are bringing some beauty into

the world, and being true to themselves,' claims Quentin.

'When's the last time you saw a happy artist?' counters Tasha.

'When's the last time you saw a happy bureaucrat?' demands John. 'I don't know why we all go along with this career thing. It's like there's these gigantic myths that we've all bought into that we can't really do what we want so we better get on with what's left over. Well, bugger it! I mean, what's the point? What is there left to be ambitious for? When people talk about being productive, what they mean is finding some new way to exploit the earth and stuff up the environment. The system that we're so busy propping up with our work and our taxes is so corrupt it makes Nixon look good. We're all getting screwed and tugging our forelocks in gratitude. Why?'

'Hang about,' objects Siobhàn. 'Weren't you the one arguing for the dignity of work a few minutes back?'

'Yeah, but that was before we started getting near the end of our morning tea-break.'

Tasha sits before the screen, deep in contemplation. Eventually she starts mousing around directories, looking for a forgotten folder. 'Poetry' it is called. It's many months since it has been opened.

She sits unmoved before her own words. Never sure if they are profound or precious. Emotions

What is the good of being a genius if you cannot use it as an excuse for being unemployed?
Gerald Barzan

cast in font; hopes frozen in binary. And is that nostalgia or regret?

Gradually the tribe assembles. Quentin, master of the culinary arts, presides. Against the odds, he is relaxed and radiant, a glass of wine slopping lazily in his hand.

The entrée plates are already at the table. A selection of late summer salad leaves is topped with strawberries and accompanied by crabmeat with a rich mustard sauce. Claire is so entranced that she kisses Quentin on the cheek.

'All right already,' pronounces Siobhàn once they are all eating. 'What is it we're up for tonight?'

'Drugs,' Quentin informs.

'Drugs?' asks Claire.

'Drugs,' agrees Quentin.

'No thanks, not while I'm drinking,' says Siobhàn. 'Maybe after the meal.'

'We're going to tackle the topic of drugs and their usage, by divine fiat of the chef,' Quentin insists. 'I want to know your considered opinions.'

'Well, you probably know where I stand,' grumps Tasha.

'We may indeed know, but we're making no assumptions,' responds Quentin. 'So perhaps you'd like to expand on that frown which is disfiguring your face.'

'I've got no time for drugs,' Tasha rules, 'or for the people who use them. It's the underbelly of Western civilization and the spotty self-indulgence of our generation. People who can't face life don't deserve the opportunity to waste it.'

'Your compassion is devastating in its absence,' judges Quentin. 'That's all of us around the table consigned to the gas chamber, I presume?'

'Pardon?'

'We're all drinking wine, as far as my limited powers of observation are able to assess. And I have it on good authority that wine contains alcohol, a drug which depresses the nervous system, induces euphoria and is potentially addictive. So presumably we're all hopeless wretches who can't face life and don't deserve the chance.'

'Don't give me that stuff. I'm talking about drugs, not a few glasses of wine with a meal. That's not in the same ball-park.'

'And why, precisely?'

'People take drugs to get high, to get out of it, to escape from reality. Unless you're an alcoholic or a miserable drunk, most people drink to enhance the pleasure of their social interaction. I've seen the downside of alcohol, so I'm not soft on it. But drug-taking is the equivalent of deliberate self-induced alcoholism.'

'On the odd occasion that I do drugs,' contributes Siobhàn, 'I do it for social interaction and all. I can't see what the difference is, truly I can't.'

'Well alcohol's legal, for a start,' Tasha argues.

'Legality's not much of an argument,' John breaks in. 'Genocide was legal in the Third Reich, and killing babies is in our time.'

'What do you mean, "killing babies"? That's a

Alcohol is like love. The first kiss is magic, the second is intimate, the third is routine. After that you take the girl's clothes off.

Raymond Chandler

damned strong term to use if it's abortion you're speaking of,' says Siobhàn angrily.

'The result's the same whatever you call it,' John mutters.

'Sidetrack, sidetrack,' calls Quentin. 'Back to drugs, please.'

'I've only ever smoked hash a couple of times,' admits Claire.

'I truly can't imagine it,' says Siobhàn. 'What happened?'

'Nothing the first time, except that I got nauseous from the tobacco. And then the second time, I rather enjoyed it. But I was very silly. I've never had any since.'

'Would you if you had the chance?' Quentin inquires.

'I think yes, probably. It didn't seem to have any bad effects. Just like a few drinks, only brighter and happier. Sorry, Tash.'

'Would you take LSD if I offered it to you?' Tasha responds.

'I wouldn't think so, no.'

'How about if you were already stoned when I offered it?'

'Perhaps then I might.'

'I rest my case,' Tasha concludes. 'A poor bloody innocent like Claire would be doing smack in a matter of months.'

'I was heavy into drugs for a while,' confesses Siobhàn. 'I had a friend, Colleen, who I used to do some art classes with, and she was dealing. So she used to give me stuff for free, you know. It was a bit of a lark; a few pills to be washed down with the Guinness, or a bit of smoke before going to a concert. I never took it too seriously. And then she started giving me speed, and it was great. I could party all night.

'But after a while, see, I started to notice that after a night of speed I was absolutely ratshit — shaking and twitching like a man pissing on our power cable. And depressed — I'd go into this black space where there was no getting out, you know what I mean? When you feel that bad then all you want is something to make you come right again, and Colleen always had something that would do the trick. So I wake up one morning with my tongue like a donkey's arse, and I can see what's happening. I just stopped like that. It was hard enough. Nowadays I mostly just have a bit of the smoke to see me through. And Guinness is always good to me.

'But Colleen, see, she just got more and more into it. I didn't see her much after I stopped needing supplies. But I heard that she'd been busted, and that she's doing probation. And then I come across her one day at the bus stop, and she looks awful. White as communion, and thin. She looked like a corpse that'd risen from the dead, I swear. Her eyes were dull as those on a stale fish. I couldn't even talk to her. She just smiled at me in a sort of superior way. It was like someone had stolen

My main experience is this: when you start taking drugs, it doesn't matter which kind. I was able to take them for a certain amount of time and hold it together somewhat. But there does come a time when, little by little, your whole body and mind will split apart and dissolve into a little puddle of piss.
Iggy Pop

her away and just left her frail little body there to wander around.

'I sometimes wonder what's happened to her; she could be dead by now for all I know. She was a beautiful girl, Colleen was.'

The main course is delivered after some final attention from Quentin. It consists of beef strips in a port marinade, stir-fried with aubergine and mushroom on a bed of turmeric-yellow rice. It is accompanied, as always, by a fresh garden salad.

> I often sit back and think 'I wish I'd done that,' and find out later that I already have.
>
> Richard Harris

'I use a variety of substances to enhance my moods,' reveals Quentin. 'Nothing intravenous and acid very rarely, but E to dance with and smoke quite often. Alcohol most of all, in a moderate way. As far as I know, I'm in good health and addicted to nothing other than *Star Trek*.'

'John is being his usual quiet self in the corner,' probes Siobhàn.

'Hmmm. Different from most of you, I guess. I didn't touch anything other than beer until quite late in the piece – mid-twenties probably. And then I did a binge thing of trying anything and everything that was going. Almost everything, anyway. Drug of choice was mescaline, though it's hard to get in lil' ol' New Zealand. Nowadays, almost nothing, except a few wines and an occasional joint.'

'I take it "a few wines" is a figure of speech?' Tasha suggests uncharitably.

'That was a bad night, Tash. I had some stuff going on I was trying to avoid.'

'Which is what, it seems to me, drugs are all about,' she reiterates.

'How about the idea that they're a form of soft technology?' Quentin proffers.

'You what?' asks Siobhàn.

'Technology is what we use to expand our universe,' he explains. 'It extends the reach of our wills and the range of options we have. Soft technology is stuff that is on a more human scale, and more deeply interactive with our minds. Virtual reality, for example. So maybe drugs are part of the development of soft technology. We already use medicinal drugs to fix things in our bodies. Recreational drugs may become ways in which we can explore different psychic states and worlds. The better we get at synthesizing particular drugs to do particular things, the more control we have over the results.

'Imagine, for example, a certain drug which enhances and binds memory cells. You could take it when you were having an especially enjoyable experience, and thereafter it would be more readily available to you. Doesn't have to be the obvious, like sex. Maybe you could take it when you went to have a last conversation with a dying relative. The possibilities are endless, especially once we start to find our way around the various brain chemicals.'

'Maybe,' says John, 'drug users are the pioneers of the new territory. The inner landscape is the

If the human race wants to go to hell in a basket, technology can help it get there by jet. It won't change the desire or the direction, but it can greatly speed the passage.
Charles M. Allen

unexplored country of the age. We might look back on druggies as the courageous adventurers who opened up the psychic spaces, and gave their lives so that we could follow in safety.'

'To boldly go where no substance had been before,' adds Quentin.

I'll die young but it's like kissing God.

Lenny Bruce

'And where no sane person would want to go again,' Tasha scoffs.

'It's like keeping a tiger for a pet,' Claire decides. 'You get friendly with it, you think it can be trusted, it follows you round wherever you go. But any day, the tiger might suddenly turn on you and kill you. It's no good blaming the tiger, because that's what tigers do. Doing drugs is a bit the same. You never know when you've overstepped the mark.'

Every now and then when your life gets complicated and the weasels start closing in, the only real cure is to load up on heinous chemicals and then drive like a bastard from Hollywood to Las Vegas.

Hunter S. Thompson

'So why do we do drugs, those of us who do? What's in it for us? Is it to get out of things or to get into things?' asks John.

'To get out of it, for me,' Quentin replies without hesitation. 'I'm a party boy, and drugs help me get down. I'm all for escapism.'

'But why?' Tasha wants to know. 'Is reality too tough for you to face?'

'It's a shit world. It's not that I can't face it, but from time to time I don't want to face it. Frankly I'd rather be somewhere else. Substance abuse gives me a way of escaping that's cheaper than overseas travel. It's a key to creating false worlds where I can live differently.'

'A bit like fiction?' asks John.

'Yes, now that you mention it. In fact I find that doing a little something from time to time helps me with my creativity.'

'Okay,' John muses, 'that's a bit closer to what I'd call going into things rather than getting out of them. My main interest in drugs is spiritual exploration,' he suggests tentatively.

'How do you work that one out?' mocks Tasha.

'No, leave him be,' Siobhàn intervenes, 'I want to hear more about this. Go on, John.'

'Well with drugs it seems to me that there's blockers and there's openers. Most of the downers work to block stuff out so that you can retreat into a comfortable womb. But the more psychoactive stuff like acid works the other way round. It opens up new vistas of experience; sensory paths that aren't normally available. Seems to me that under certain conditions, these sorts of drugs can project people into an instant awareness of the spiritual.'

'So how come I just get to have a good time?' Quentin asks. 'Is it because I'm unspiritual or just because I can't afford the good gear?'

'Maybe you just don't name it the same. Let's say you go to a dance party and do some E. It's a great night, and you feel so close to this group of people, like there was some sort of cosmic oneness, and your dancing was part of the response to that.'

'Sounds familiar,' Quentin agrees. 'Go on.'

'Now maybe you put it down to the drug, and

No monster vibration, no snake universe hallucinations. Many tiny jewelled violet flowers along the path of a living brook that looked like Blake's illustration for a canal in grassy Eden: huge Pacific watery shore, Orlovsky dancing naked like Shiva long-haired before giant green waves, titanic cliffs that Wordsworth mentioned in his own Sublime, great yellow sun veiled with mist hanging over the planet's oceanic horizon. No harm.

think, "Man, where can I get some more of that stuff?" But have you ever considered that the drug is not producing the experience at all? That all that the E is doing is taking away the normal barriers to perception? What's happening is that you're picking up the vibes which are coming from the event itself. It's the gathering of the tribe and their celebration which is significant, and the gear simply helps you to hook into the feelings which are being generated.'

'So why do we need the drugs to experience it?' Siobhàn asks.

'That,' says John, 'is certainly the question.'

'I had this experience on acid one time,' Siobhàn tells, 'that I've never talked about. No laughing now,' as she threatens with her eyes.

'I was staying in an old farmhouse with a bunch of friends from Dublin. We went up for the weekend, and we had some good stuff, so we all dropped tabs on the Sunday morning. I went out for a walk on my own, up into the hills. I came across this flat spot where it looked as though there had been a building of some sort. There was a big stone thing that had broken off and was lying on the ground. Anyway, I sit down there for a rest and the trip really comes on, you know?

'And all of a sudden I can hear music. Beautiful lilting voices singing plainsong, chanting like. And it's the old language they're using. I close my eyes to listen to it, and when I open them again, there's people moving around, dressed in robes. It wasn't scary or anything – it just seemed kind of natural, as if they belonged there. I'm trying to work out what it is they're doing, and it seems to be some sort of ritual. The stone that was lying broken is somehow standing again. All their movements are in relation to the thing.

'I want to join in, and so I raise my voice and start singing, and suddenly I've got the Irish and the words and I'm doing harmony with the rest of them. One of the monk people stops and turns around to look at me. Only I can't see his face, 'cos it's shadowed by this big hood thing he's wearing. But he seems to be looking right into my soul. And then he speaks to me, speaks without making any sound. "Siobhàn," he says, "you've lost your way. The light shines and you turn away. Find the light, and it will make the way clear."

'That was it, really. It all faded as quickly as it had come, and I was left with the usual acid stuff. But it got under my skin, you know? It somehow seemed more real than reality. That voice kept ringing in my head for weeks afterwards. Sometimes even now I wake up and I know I've been hearing the same words again in my sleep.'

'That's creepy,' Claire shudders.

'That's certifiable,' Tasha dismisses. 'Druggie hallucinations. They'd call it psychosis in another time, and lock you up.'

'Dessert,' announces Quentin.

It is a secret concoction of baked caramel, accompanied by a chocolate sauce and cream.

> Nobody stopped thinking about those psychedelic experiences. Once you've been to some of those places, you think, 'How can I get back there but make it a little easier on myself?'
> Jerry Garcia

'I may or may not have laced the sauce with various hallucinogenic substances,' teases Quentin. 'The proof lies in the eating.'

'I hope there's enough for seconds,' grins Siobhàn eagerly.

'What I want to know,' Quentin insists,' is why escapism has such a bad press. None of us handle reality well enough to want to live there all the time. Everyone has their own way of getting out of it for a little relief.'

'I'm not sure that I do,' protests Claire.

'With all due respect, my lovely, the rare exception in your case is when you tune *in* to reality.'

'What's that supposed to mean?'

'Darling, you're on another planet. It may well be a higher form of evolution, but to the rest of us poor mortals it resembles a trance-like state. You exist in some private world of reverie, and poke your head out periodically like a tortoise.'

'My mother always called me dreamy. But I don't see what that has to do with drugs.'

'It's a form of escape, that's all. Some people watch movies, others go jogging for endorphin highs, and some special people retreat inside their heads for a little innocent daydreaming. My point is that all of them are withdrawing from the cold hard facts of "the real world". If I occasionally use a little chemical assistance to achieve the same end, what's the difference? It's only one of method; maybe style. As they used to say, "whatever turns you on".'

'It's artificial, though, isn't it? You're playing around with brain chemicals without really knowing how they work. You could be doing all sorts of damage to your genes or something,' Claire argues.

'Nothing that the Laundromat won't fix,' Quentin responds.

'Hang on, I'm not wearing this bullshit,' Tasha rejoins the fray.

'Which particular part of the bovine excrement are you wanting to discard?' teases Quentin.

'Look, I'm prepared to admit that we've all got tendencies to escape from the real world. I know I do it from time to time with computers. But let's not make it into a bloody virtue. The fact is that every withdrawal from life is a failure. Whenever we step back from the front lines, whenever we disengage, it's because we're not tough enough to take it. Growing up, becoming adult, is a matter of leaving behind fantasy and accepting reality. So even if I do escape from time to time, I recognize it as a sort of immaturity; a failure to be really present in the world. Recommending retreat through drugs is just a big wank – a return to the primal womb to sulk.'

'All right, already,' John gets enlivened. 'But tell me now, which is the real world? It's a myth, isn't it? It doesn't really exist. No one has direct access to it. All we have is these filtered impressions which come through our senses, and then we imprint them with meaning. Half of it dredged up from our unconscious mind, the other half

Illusions are art, for the feeling person, and it is by art that we live.

Elizabeth Bowen

regulated by societal consensus. I'm always suspicious of calls to live in the real world. Half the time it's a hidden attempt to insist that everyone lives according to someone else's rules.'

'What a lot of tossing rubbish!' Tasha sneers. 'Do you think starving people sit around debating whether they have access to the real world or not? Maybe these hunger pains in our stomachs are an illusion? Nah, reality is what gets up and bites you in the face. Everyone shares it, unless they're off in some bloody social workers' twilight zone.'

'How about Siobhàn's story, then?' counters John. 'Did it really happen or not?'

'Of course it didn't happen! It was an *illusion*. You know, that's when you think that things are happening, but they're not really happening at all, because they're caused by the chemical junk that's floating around in your brain. Most people who have those sort of experiences are termed psychiatrically ill, but for some unknown reason self-inflicted abuse of the mind is not included in that category as yet.'

'But how can you possibly *know*? What if it was really happening? It could be a dimension which is always there, but which we're blind to most of the time. So taking drugs opened Siobhàn's eyes to something which was really there. Maybe the world she looked into was more real than the everyday world we take for granted. Maybe the message she received was of more use to her than what she reads in the paper every morning.'

'Yeah, and maybe the supposed monk might

have told her that she had wings and could fly. But if she stepped off the top of a tall building, she would have found out which world was the most real, wouldn't she?'

'She might have hit the ground and died. And maybe she would have found the monk waiting for her.'

'Now you're just being ridiculous. If you want to get into quasi-mystical mumbo jumbo, then I need to bow out. None of it is half as real to me as the fact that the dishes have got to be done.'

'In that case,' says Siobhàn, 'I'm with John.'

Quentin and Siobhàn leave the others clearing up, and head off for a walk through the park. It is one of those early autumn nights when the coolness is welcome. They stop to sit on a bench near the pond.

'It's a strange thing, now, Quentin, but all that talk of drugs has left me wanting to get just a little bit out of it.'

'As it happens, I might just have the makings of something here in my pocket,' he says, producing a tobacco tin and shaking it promisingly.

'If you're not a saint, then you're just a whisker short of canonization. Or maybe it's a whisky short. God bless you and hurry up and make it.'

A silence descends as Quentin is absorbed in his craft of construction. Siobhàn leans her head back over the bench and regards the night sky. It's hard to make out the stars with the glare of the city lights.

A drug is neither moral nor immoral – it's a chemical compound. The compound itself is not a menace to society until a human being treats it as if consumption bestowed a temporary licence to act like an asshole.

Frank Zappa

'It's not such a bad old world,' she admits, 'with the earth under your feet and the sky for a ceiling. I wish I didn't feel cut off from it so much, you know what I mean?'

'Umph,' Quentin agrees, deep in toke.

'I sometimes suspect it must have some meaning to it. But that's only on my bad days. Here, give us a suck, will you? I feel like getting wiggly.'

Chapter Eight

It is mostly dark as John wakes, with only the hint of dawn. The early morning is a lacuna midway between states of consciousness. In it there is a gap worthy of exploration.

John wraps a robe around himself, and fumbles under the bed to remove a rough wooden kneeler. An old friend made it for him. He settles himself onto it, and lights the candle. It flares and steadies, a single pure light in the darkness. His breathing slows, and he slips easily into the rhythms of prayer.

There is nothing to be seen. A candle burning in the gloom; a body stilled apart from breath; a silence almost womb-like.

Prayer is translation. A man translates himself into a child asking for all there is in a language he has barely mastered.

Leonard Cohen

Tasha is unsettled in her sleep; the bedclothes tortured into disarray. The dream lurks heavily in the background. Siobhàn's monk, laughing. Not in derision, but heartily. The sound of it rings in her ears. He came to her across the fields. 'Who are you?' she asked. 'I'm he who lives in your imagination,' he replied. 'What do you want?' Tasha demanded. 'Recognition,' was all he said. And then he began chuckling, and it went on and on. She wanted to join in, but it somehow seemed like a betrayal, and so she just smiled. 'I don't even believe in you,' she said to herself.

There is something naïve and nostalgic about the sound of a fountain-pen on paper. Quentin enjoys the sensation, independently of anything he may be writing.

As it happens, it's a letter. An exercise for the writers' group. He pauses and sucks on the pen, reviewing what he's produced thus far.

Dear Philip,

Thanks for the invite to join you and others for the *Self-Transformation* weekend, which the promotional literature describes as an opportunity for 'confronting truth' and 'releasing divine energy'. I wish you all well on your voyage into the interior.

Unfortunately I will not be joining you on this pilgrimage. I suppose I could produce some convincing excuse by way of another engagement, but to do so would not be entirely honest. The truth of the matter is that I have an extreme reaction against group processes, and in particular those which engender emotional release or intimate revelation. I realize this makes me quaintly old-fashioned, and may even be evidence of some sort of 'blockage', but there you have it.

I also react badly to the confusion of boundaries between friendship and commerce. Ever since an old friend of mine invited me for dinner and I arrived to find myself at a seminar for the promotion of cleaning products, I have regarded such transgressions as possibly the most pernicious invasion of capitalism yet devised. Of course I hold out the hope that your reason for sending me this material was a heartfelt concern for the state of my soul, and nothing to do with your membership of this new group. But all in all I wish you hadn't sent it. It casts a shadow of doubt over our friendship which I am finding difficult to erase.

You might recall that last night in Paris when we walked together alongside the Seine. I was not entirely sober, but I still remember the course of our conversation. You were searching for meaning; I for love. You wanted insight; I craved intimacy. You hoped for enlightenment; I was ready to settle for entanglement. What happened I put down to the air of Paris, which is a form of gaseous lust disguised as romance. No matter – in the short term my needs were fulfilled and yours were not.

I look back on it as the parting of our ways. I remain unsure whether your new spiritual quest is the flowering of the things you spoke of that night, or a reaction against the events which followed. It seems to me that you retain an almost Calvinist strand of moral purity, and that the sort of encounter group you have subsequently been drawn to may act as a form of confessional. I hope I am wrong, and that your current investigations are motivated by the longing for salvation rather than the fear of damnation. Personally, my own conscience is cleansed by love, even though that love be recently unrequited.

On an entirely different matter, I have some bad news for you. My latest test results have come back positive, and my whole future has been cast into uncertainty. This has obvious implications for you, and I am deeply sorry for them. Certainly, for me, this news has been 'self-transformation' enough, though without the compensation of divine energy...

Sometimes I have a terrible feeling that I am dying not from the virus, but from being untouchable.
Amanda Heggs

Quentin smiles and ponders. It should make quite a hit in the circle.

··········

'There's a package arrived for you,' Siobhàn informs her. 'I put it on the table.'

'Thanks,' is all the response Claire gives, smiling.

'Well, go on. Open it up. I can't stand the mystery.'

'I'll open it later – there's no hurry,' demurs Claire.

'Bollocks you will. I have to go out, and I want to know why you're getting parcels sent to you.'

'It'll be from my parents.'

'And?'

Claire drops her head and her face colours. 'It's my birthday,' she says.

'Aaagh,' squeals Siobhàn, throwing her arms around Claire and dancing her around the room. 'Happy birthday, you daft lump. Why didn't you let us know? We'll have to have a party now.'

'Can't. I'm meeting my parents for dinner.'

'What's all the noise?' asks John, emerging from the hall.

'It's Claire's birthday,' reveals Siobhàn. 'We need to celebrate, only she's going out tonight.'

'Happy whatevers,' says John, kissing Claire discreetly on the cheek. 'Let's make it Friday night. We can have a birthday dinner.'

'Great idea,' proclaims Siobhàn. 'Why don't we all go out for a change? Then no one has to cook. Claire?'

'I suppose so. I've kept Friday free anyway for our usual get-together.'

At twenty you have many desires which hide the truth, but beyond forty there are only real and fragile truths – your abilities and your failings.

Gerard Depardieu

'Excellent,' says John. 'Truly excellent.'

'Now open the parcel so we can all see,' insists Siobhàn.

It's a down-at-heel Italian place, by the inevitable name of Mario's. The food and price compensate for the lack of ambience. They've booked the round table in the front window, which means they can all talk and watch the world go by. Siobhàn has secretly informed the staff that it's Claire's birthday.

The waiter is a genuine Italian in a white shirt and black waistcoat. He is fiftyish, with a grey moustache and an amiably wrinkled brow. He looks as though he could serve your pasta or arrange the death of your enemy with equal nonchalance. On Quentin's advice, he ignores Claire's order for a lime and bitters, instead bringing a bottle of champagne. Her protestations are suavely circumvented as he pours a little into her glass.

'Here's to St Claire,' proposes Siobhàn. 'The best hour of the day to you, the best day of the week to you, the best week of the year to you, the best year of your life to you.'

'Speech, speech,' calls Quentin.

'Oh no, please not,' Claire pleads, hiding behind her hands.

'Tell us a story, then. Something about your growing up.'

Claire might have continued to protest, were it not for the united chorus of approval against her. She uncharacteristically tosses back her champagne

A good story cannot be devised; it has to be distilled.
Raymond Chandler

and digs into the past, emerging eventually with a rusting treasure.

'One summer we took our holidays in the Cotswolds. Daddy had hired a little cottage, and we stayed there for a couple of weeks. It was a beautiful place – the birds and the flowers. I was about eight, I suppose – no older, anyway. Every day seemed perfect, and my parents were as happy as I've ever seen them. There was a hill behind the cottage, and a little stream at the bottom. I spent most of my days down there, wandering around, lying in the sun, putting my feet in the water, finding treasures to bring home to Mummy.

'One afternoon I walked further than usual, following the course of the stream. I came across a fence with a stile over it, and climbed over into the neighbouring property. I could hear voices in the distance, and I suppose I must have been curious as to who was there. I crept through the trees and eventually came to a house. The trees were quite close to a window, and I could see inside clearly. A man and a woman were arguing – shouting at each other. The man was using vile language, and I cringed back against a tree, frightened. The woman, who I guessed was his wife, alternated between crying and yelling at him.

'I couldn't make much sense of the conversation because her voice was quieter than his. And then quite suddenly, he hit her. I'd never seen a man hit a woman before, and it all took place in slow motion. It wasn't just a slap; it was a full roundhouse blow with his fist which caught

Violence is one of the most fun things to watch.
Quentin Tarantino

152

her on the side of the face and knocked her over. I was shocked and angry and scared all at the same time. I didn't know what I should do. The man seemed to be suddenly overcome with remorse. He helped his wife to her feet, but she had blood on her face and was sobbing inconsolably.

'When things had quietened down somewhat, I went home. I didn't say anything to my parents, because I knew they'd be angry at me for being a peeping Tom. A few days later, there was a knock on the door and Daddy ushered in the same man. Only now he was wearing a black shirt with a white collar on. Daddy introduced him as the vicar doing the village rounds. I couldn't get out of the room fast enough, and offered to help Mummy make the cup of tea. She left to go back into the other room for a while, leaving me in charge of the preparations.

'I think I must have been in a state of shock. I kept seeing that blow to his wife's face, and comparing it to the jolly, polite man who was presently ensconced in our front room. In the medicine cupboard were some Epsom salts. I made some room on one side of the sugar bowl, and poured in a heap of the dreaded salts. Then when the tea was taken through and poured, I kindly offered the sugar around. The vicar was deeply engrossed in whatever Daddy was saying, and hardly noticed as I used the teaspoon to shovel two spoons of Epsom salts into his tea. Of course for my parents I took it from the genuinely sugary side of the bowl.

'From the first mouthful he knew something

> The priesthood is a marriage. People often start by falling in love, and they go on for years without realizing that that love must change into some other love which is so unlike it that it can hardly be recognized as love at all.
> Iris Murdoch

was wrong. But what could he say? Perhaps this was the way that my mother made tea – the others seemed to be drinking it without any problem. He was too polite to complain. It was all I could do to keep a straight face while he made his way through the cup. And surprise, surprise, he had to cut short his visit and be on his way. Pressing business, he said. Later when I was alone I laughed and laughed, and felt wicked and guilty at the same time. I shouldn't have done it, but it gave me such a lot of pleasure that I still enjoy it now.'

The laughter and the champagne create a glow around the table. The mood is only enhanced with the arrival of the entrees. Claire's remembering seems to have released something within her, and she is vivacious and enchanting. All this John observes as if he were at a distance, looking on. There is a moistness in his eye.

'So what's our topic for tonight?' Siobhàn wants to know.

'Oh god, we're not going to have a discussion *here*, are we?' whines Tasha.

'Absolutely,' Quentin enthuses. 'It's Friday night, and that means it's time for issues. I guess it should be Claire's chance to choose, seeing she's the star.'

'Pass,' grins Claire. 'I can totally assure you I have nothing whatsoever on my mind tonight.' And she seems to be looking at John as she says it.

Or that's how it seems to Siobhàn in one of those fleeting impressions.

'How about abortion?' asks Siobhàn.

'No thanks; I'll settle for Parmesan,' quips Quentin.

'We're definitely not talking abortion,' insists Tasha. 'I've had a gutful of that subject and we'd only end up shouting at each other.'

'What about ageing?' John proposes.

'A bit morbid, isn't it?' counters Tasha. 'Here we all are in the prime of our youth, and you want to pull the rug out from under us.'

'No, I think it has possibilities,' says Siobhàn. 'Lead on, Johnny-boy.'

Claire is just smiling.

Ageing seems to be the only available way to live a long life.
Daniel F.E. Auber

'Seems to me,' John begins, 'that the very worst thing that can happen to anyone in today's world is for them to grow old. Look at the size of the industry that we've produced to work against the ageing process. Plastic surgery, cosmetics, health clubs; all of them vying against nature in the vain hope of holding on to youth. It may well be the dumbest thing that humanity has ever attempted. I keep thinking of those drug couriers who swallow condoms full of heroin and then get caught by the police. They try to sit it out – not eating and hoping against hope that they won't shit. But no matter how long they can hold out, eventually the truth and the heroin emerges. Some things it's just not worth fighting against.

'But the worst part of it is the culture of

Women have face-lifts in a society in which women without them appear to vanish from sight.
Naomi Wolf

uselessness it produces in older people. Young is beautiful, strong, sexy, intelligent, fast. Old is weak, ugly, dull, slow, reactionary. All of a sudden thirty-year-olds are beginning to wonder if they're past their peak. The only hope is to carry off the illusion of youth for as long as you can, in order to enjoy the benefits of it. It's such a crazy view of life. We despise the very thing that we're all going to become. There was a time when age was honoured and youth dismissed, and now we've totally turned the tables. There's no respect left for the elders of our community. They're just a burden on the economy, a drain on the health budget.

'Personally I think age is like gravity – you can fight against it all you like but it's not going to go away. Much better to find ways of using it to your advantage than resisting the process. The whole culture is youth-obsessed, and it gets more and more ridiculous every year. People cutting up their bodies in order to look younger than they really are is a form of obscenity in my view. So, as far as I'm concerned, getting older is something to be accepted and celebrated; and I'm glad we're doing just that here with Claire tonight.'

'Easy for you to say,' challenges Claire.
'What d'you mean?'
'Well, the whole thing's different for women and men, isn't it? By and large, men are considered more attractive the older they get, whereas for women it's the exact opposite. Beauty is our most

> Growing old's like being increasingly penalized for a crime you haven't committed.
>
> Anthony Powell

156

important asset, but it only flowers for such a short period, and then begins to fade. We lose what's most precious to us. Ageing is just a downhill process for women, while for a lot of men they're on the up and up.'

'Yeah, go for it, Claire,' cheers Siobhàn. 'These bastard men can go on and on about the dignity of older women, and then they ditch their forty-year-old wives for some nubile bimbo in the office. Face up to it, John: for women getting old is about bleeding to death slowly.'

'Hang about,' protests John. 'All you're saying is that most people, both men and women, have bought into the "youth equals beauty" equation. But that doesn't make it right. I find older people genuinely beautiful in a way that has some depth, because I'm looking at them differently.'

'Yeah, but would you bonk a seventy-year-old woman?' demands Siobhàn.

A fleeting look of horror ripples across John's face, betraying him and answering the question.

'Anyone heard of the Physically Immortals?' asks Tasha.

'No, but tell us, darling,' enthuses Quentin.

'They're a bunch of nutters from the West Coast of America, who believe that ageing and death are all in the mind. They're convinced that if you can just get past societal conditioning which programmes you to get old, then you can stay as young as you like for as long as you like. So long in fact that you never die. Death is just

> It is not all bad, this getting old, ripening. After the fruit has got its growth it should juice up and mellow. God forbid I should live long enough to ferment and rot and fall to the ground in a squash.
> Emily Carr

wrong thinking, you see. You only need to change your mind about it; believe that you will live for ever and it will come to pass. Naturally enough it's a reasonably young movement. And they don't have life membership.'

'Yes, but that's Americans,' explains Claire.

'It seems to me that it's the natural extension of what John's talking about,' Tasha continues. 'Ageing and dying are such awful concepts to everyone that we just blot them out altogether and pretend they don't happen.'

'I guess the movement's not big among funeral directors,' reflects Quentin.

'I read somewhere that scientists have identified the gene which causes ageing,' Tasha reports. 'So in theory it might be possible to drastically slow and even stop the ageing process in the not too distant future.'

'But would you want it?' asks John. 'I think I'd find the prospect of eternal youth enough of a bore, without contemplating eternal life. One of the most intriguing parts of life is growth and development – perpetual youth is the absence of growth. The bloody world's run by enough arrogant brats as it is.'

'Does growth and development include decay?' inquires Siobhàn.

'Yeah, of course it does. Everything has a life-span. It's young and immature, it comes to the fullness of its expression, and then it begins to fade away. You can no more hold on to the middle

Most people think that ageing is irreversible and we know that there are mechanisms even in the human machinery that allow for the reversal of ageing, through correction of diet, through antioxidants, through removal of toxins from the body, through exercise, through yoga and breathing techniques, and through meditation.

Deepak Chopra

bit than you can catch the wind. It's a lost cause, and I don't know what the motivation is, anyway.'

'Oh I don't know — things like being active, attractive and witty may have something to do with it,' suggests Quentin. 'As opposed to getting senile and bedridden.'

'Anyway, I'm not that old,' declares Claire. 'You'd think I was turning fifty, the way you lot are going on.'

John rushes to atone. 'Sorry, sorry, sorry. I'm not meaning to make connections with your birthday in all this. You're so lovely, Claire, that no one in their right mind would…'

'Carry on, John — you were saying?' teases Siobhàn.

His face has flushed a little and he is examining the tines on his fork. Claire appears nonchalant, but her eyes are shining. Fortunately the main courses arrive to interrupt further group speculation.

'Birthdays are a mixed blessing,' Quentin asserts between mouthfuls of pasta. 'I always feel that they should be more important than they turn out to be.'

'How so?' asks Tasha.

'Coming to the end of one year of your life and starting off on another seems like it should be of enormous significance. It's a point of transition; a mountaintop in the topography of life from which you should be able to look back and forward. But in the end it turns out to be a celebration with

I don't believe one grows older. I think that what happens early on in life is that at a certain age one stands still and stagnates.

T.S. Eliot

The older you get the stronger the wind gets — and it's always in your face.

Jack Nicklaus

your friends, and you wake up in the morning feeling not much different from the day before. It's all a bit of a let-down, really.'

'Thanks a lot,' groans Claire.

'Oh, not your birthday, silly. Here we all are having a fabulous time with scintillating conversation and good food. No, I was speaking in regard to *moi*, as usual. I seem to be psychologically incapable of rising to occasions.'

'There's some birthdays I want to forget,' says Tasha quietly.

'Tell, tell,' insists Quentin.

'I'd just graduated when I turned twenty-one,' she begins. 'I had my first job, and it seemed like a good opportunity for a celebration. We organized a party in my flat. I invited everyone I knew – a lot of university friends, and people from work. The night started out swimmingly, and the place was pumping. I knocked back a couple of quick glasses of bubbly, and everything was looking wonderful. And then Robbie turned up.

'He was going through a punk phase, so he had his hair spiked in alternate stripes of orange and blue. His face gleamed with bits of metal stuck through every spare bit of flesh. There was a parting of the waves as he entered the room, people shrinking back, uncertain what to make of him. He had a girl with him, Ziggy her name was. She had a charming black dress on, covered with bits of chainmail from which she'd hung tampons. Her head was completely shaved.

'I didn't know what to do. I was so embarrassed, but he was my brother, after all, and I loved him dearly. I knew what sort of stuff he'd had to put up with at home, whereas everyone else could only see what was on the outside. There was this moment of shocked silence when he walked up to me with everyone watching. I think they imagined I was about to be raped or murdered or something. He threw his arms around me and picked me up and whirled me around. Our laughing together broke the tension, and people sighed and went back to their conversations.

'It was all a bit too emotional for me, and I must have drunk more than I usually do. By the time it came to speeches later in the night, I was a little unsteady and had started slurring my words. I thanked everyone for coming and said what a special night it was; all the usual things you say at these things. And then I meant to say that life had been something of a battle for me, but it came out that life had been a *bottle* for me. Everyone laughed, and a guy from work with a smart mouth made some wisecrack — I didn't even hear it properly — something about whisky and frisky.

'I saw it all in slow motion. Robbie's eyes narrowed and I wanted to stop him but it was too late. He just turned and head-butted the guy, as casual as you like. The poor bloke just crumpled in a heap on the floor with blood pouring out of his nose. Some of his friends grabbed Robbie by the shoulders as he was about to put the boot in,

Perhaps violence, like pornography, is some kind of an evolutionary standby system, a last-resort device for throwing a wild joker into the game?
J.G. Ballard

161

and then all hell broke loose. There were bodies flying everywhere and furniture breaking and people screaming. I still remember that horrible flat sound of fists hitting flesh. It only lasted a couple of minutes, but by the time it was over it looked like a war zone.

'Robbie stood looking like a stupid ape with blood all over his face from a gash on his head. He was grinning at me. I started punching him in the chest and yelling at him, but he held me off at arm's length and looked at me like a mournful dog. "I was only looking out for you, Tash," he said. We both burst into tears then. People couldn't leave the place fast enough. They thought it was a madhouse. I thought I could keep my worlds separate – the past and the future – but it didn't work out. I realized the next day that my past was always going to be peering over the fence.'

'This may not sound connected, but it is,' provides Quentin by way of preamble. 'I've often thought that one of the problems with our society is that we've lost the power of rites of passage. If you look at ancient societies, they have elaborate rituals to mark important points of transition, like from childhood to adulthood. They're highly public things in which the whole community recognizes that something has shifted in relation to an individual, and that nothing will be the same for them again. But what do we have? Nothing. And so you get these young guys roaming around with adult bodies but they're still big kids at heart. They've neither let go of their childhood nor accepted the new responsibilities of being an adult.'

'Oh god, he's been reading Robert Bly. We'll be dancing naked round the campfire in a minute,' Siobhàn mocks.

'No, listen. All this acting out of violence by adolescent males – fist fights and rapes and so on – is an attempt to get some sort of recognition. Kids are trying to say "I've arrived; I'm one of the big people; notice me." There's no accepted staging post for them, so they have to go racing in cars or killing cats or something to demonstrate their manhood.'

'There might be something in it,' concedes Siobhàn. 'But it's not just a male thing, is it now? For girls it's the same. I guess we have our periods as a marker, but that's hardly a public event, thanks be to God. So it gets to be sex that marks the border. "Going all the way," as the girls used to say. That's not public either, but the talking about it damn near gets to be. You're not part of the in-group until you've screwed some lad down by the river.'

'How did we get from my birthday to teenage sex?' Claire protests.

'It's your feminine mystique,' suggests Quentin.

The waiter arrives bearing fire. He holds aloft the requested chocolate cake emblazoned with

The big mistake that men make is that when they turn thirteen or fourteen and all of a sudden they've reached puberty, they believe that they like women. Actually, you're just horny.

Jules Feiffer

candles, and a ragged chorus of 'Happy Birthday' breaks out. Claire is embarrassed and pleased in equal measure. People at surrounding tables join in the applause and merriment.

Quentin produces a package wrapped in silver paper, with a card. 'It's from us all,' he says, kissing her. Claire beams.

She unwraps the gift, which turns out to be a bedside clock. After all the appropriate noises of gratitude, Claire wipes her eyes with her fingers and clears her throat.

'You've all been perfectly lovely to me. Thanks for making my birthday really special, even if it was a few days ago. And for including me, and making me feel a part of whatever's going on. I know I get a bit dreamy sometimes, but these evenings have got to be very precious to me, and I love you all a lot. Thanks.'

'And now, back to teenage sex,' suggests Siobhàn with glee.

'I've been thinking,' muses John, 'about the sinking lid.'

'Is this some oblique reference to the ceiling, or are you going to explain for the telepathically challenged?' jibes Tasha.

'I agree with what Quentin was saying about rites of passage. It seems to me that because we've got no agreed points of transition, that adulthood is a sort of sinking lid. Talking about teenage sex highlights the problem. Kids are becoming sexually active at younger and younger ages. What used to be fifteen-year-olds getting pregnant are now twelve- or thirteen-year-olds. Same thing with drugs and violence. Every generation feels that they have to get into stuff earlier and earlier to prove that they're ahead of the last lot that went through. I wonder if there's any limit to how low it can go? And what happens to childhood and innocence? It gets squeezed out by descending maturity.'

'I was sexually active by the age of thirteen,' says Siobhàn.

'And were you ready for it?' asks John.

'I've got nothing to compare it with. I was ahead of some of my friends, but not all of them. It was just something to do, like for a dare. I never enjoyed it much, but it seemed to keep the boys happy. I grew up fast, I suppose, but that's the way it happens at home. Inside all of us we keep a little bit of childhood, and we never let it go as long as we live. I've never been scared of ageing myself — I think we maybe look after our old a little better in Ireland. My gran will still lift her skirts at a party, and nobody minds.'

'It scares the shit out of me, I don't mind admitting,' Tasha reveals. 'I use all the potions I can find, and if I have to get my skin stretched to pull the wrinkles out, then I'll be up for that as well.'

'You'll have your navel for a dimple,' offers Quentin, 'like those horrid American women whose faces are like pigskin tightened over an apple core.'

No doubt about it: teenagers — in some senses, at any rate — ripen more quickly than they used to.
Colin MacInnes

Look at the movie stars, they took the skin from their ass and stuck it on their face. The skin on their ass was the last to wrinkle. They all walked around in their later years with buttock faces.
Charles Bukowski

'Better than enlarged prostates and nasal forests,' retorts Tasha.

It's late when they get home. John makes some coffee, but all except Claire wander off for bed. She sits at the table, watching John's precise movements and smiling. He turns to find her staring. She is radiant tonight; whether it's the wine or the light or her birthday, there is a definite glow.

'You look happy, Claire.'

'It's been a wonderful night. I like being the centre of attention. I wish it happened more often.'

'I can't imagine that it doesn't.'

'How do you mean?'

'As I started to say over dinner, you're one of the most lovely people I've ever known. Whenever you walk into a room, people turn to look at you. You must be aware of it.'

'Sometimes people have told me that I'm beautiful, that I should do modelling, that sort of thing. But I never believe them. There's always a reason to dismiss what they're saying. And when I look in the mirror, all I'm aware of is my faults.'

'Do you believe it when I say it?'

'I think you've had champagne, a good meal, and everything looks good to you. And maybe some of what you're seeing is what you want to see.'

There's a few moments of silence as John turns to push the plunger in the coffee.

I have a horror of people who speak about the beautiful. What is the beautiful?

Pablo Picasso

'John?'

'Mmm?'

'There's something I'd like you to do to finish my birthday for me.'

'Yes?'

'Come to bed with me.'

The bed is now as public as the dinner table, and governed by the same rules of formal confrontation.

Angela Carter

Chapter Nine

The house is very familiar. He knows the layout, the doors, and what lies behind each of them. It's the staircase descending from the hallway which draws him. Gliding downward in the comfortable silence.

He enters the open door at the bottom, and turns to survey the room. Things have changed. On the couch sits Claire, but she is a child; perhaps ten years old. She is curled up with her thumb in her mouth, watching him. In another chair sits Siobhàn, leafing idly through a magazine. She looks up, her eyes blazing. In the corner is an upright skeleton, adorned with a black cassock.

'Be careful where you step,' says a voice neither inside nor outside the room. It is only then that he becomes aware that in the centre of the room there is a black whirlpool, foaming and roaring.

One of the characteristics of the dream is that nothing surprises us in it.

Jean Cocteau

John leaps backward, and in that instant wakes. The dawn light filters through the window in an unfamiliar way. He lies there for some minutes, rigid. The dream still holds him, more real than the light. In the near distance, someone is breathing. Claire. Slowly he allows himself to subside once more into sleep.

Claire sighs so deeply that it wakes her. Sunlight is streaming into the room, cubing the air with its suspended dust. She runs her fingers lightly over her face, which is tingling. John breathes steadily beside her. Quietly and gently, she jacks herself up on one elbow to watch him.

He has a rough innocence; larrikin good looks. She has no regrets. Sunlight is shining on one of his shoulders, revealing a tiny mole. She lowers herself to the pillow again, and snuggles against him.

The pleasures of the flesh. It's a phrase which meanders across the foreground of her mind, emerging from some forgotten recess. How deeply pleasurable they are. This languid satisfaction, it seeps to the marrow of the bone. It shrugs off morality with ease. Like sun warming the body, it produces torpor.

In love, as in gluttony, pleasure is a matter of the utmost precision.
Italo Calvino

'Morning,' mumbles John as one eyelid flicks open.

Claire doesn't answer, but leans across to kiss him softly on the cheek.

'Mmmm. How did this happen?' he wonders.

'I asked you here, and you were gracious enough to agree.'

'Gracious? I would have had ice in my veins to say no. I must have considered it at some stage, but I can't honestly say I remember. Are you okay?'

'I'm better than that. I'm satiated.' She brushes her lips across his. 'Don't look so concerned. I'm not quite as fragile as you think.'

'I'm sorry, Claire. I mean I'm not sorry about last night, which was absolutely bloody fantastic. But I'm sorry because... because it all just happened without talking or thinking, and now here I am messing up your bed, let alone your life.'

'If we had have talked about it, it might never have happened. And you may not have thought about it, but I certainly have. I wouldn't have asked you otherwise.'

'I don't think I ever seriously considered the possibility. It seemed too impossible – like wanting to climb Mount Everest, or having a crush on Sharon Stone or something. You're so far out of my orbit, Claire.'

'What do you mean?'

'You're lovely and gentle and kind and beautiful. And I'm an ugly rude Antipodean bloke, charging around stepping over everyone's boundaries and social conventions. I feel vulgar next to you.'

'Perhaps that's what makes you so attractive,' she smiles. 'Your brute vulgarity. Anyway, it's not true and you know it. You're as soft as, underneath all the bluster.'

'Parts of me aren't at all at present,' he grins. 'But the problem is: where does this leave us?'

'Naked in bed together, I should think.'

'But it's all so complicating, isn't it? I mean, what happens after this? Do we just go back to being flatmates? And if so, what does that make this – casual sex? Or do we accept it as the start of some sort of relationship thingy, and if so what shape is it?'

'Do we need to analyse it? Can't we just enjoy it?'

170

'I don't know, Claire, I don't know. No, of course we don't have to pick it apart or sift it for meaning. But we can't ignore it, either. Sex changes things. Whatever happens from here on in, we have this *event* which is going to influence all of our interactions. I wish I was the kind of guy – no I don't, I'm glad I'm not. What I'm trying to say is that it's very hard for me to climb out of your bed, say "Ta very much" and get on with life as if it never happened. I'm already too fond of you for that.'

'I know that. If I didn't trust you I would never have invited you in the first place. I didn't just ask you to bed because I wanted a quick screw on my birthday, John. I'd be happy to explore a relationship, but I don't know what sort or how long or what the boundaries are. I'm not sure how you *can* know when you're just starting out.'

'Okay, okay. I'm happy to live with that. I'm a little scared, is all. Scared because I don't know what's involved, and scared because I'm not sure if I'm ready for it. But it sure as hell is a nice predicament to be in, and I'm honoured to be in it with you.'

'John,' she says, reaching for him, 'has anyone ever told you you talk too much?'

While she's away in the shower, John lies perfectly still, examining himself. The long fingers of conscience probe into the fleshy parts of his psyche, picking at loose strands of motivation. One word is echoing down some distant corridor.

> A relationship, I think, is like a shark, you know? It has to constantly move forward or it dies.
> Woody Allen

Hypocrite!

All your words and ideals; so eloquent, so admirable, so superficial. At least Siobhàn's honest. She doesn't pretend to anything other than who she is. Your high and mighty principles seem small enough to carry in your scrotum. Here you are with Claire's juices still damp on you. What of your commitments, your covenants, your self-respect? It's the same thing, over and over again, isn't it? Like a tiger who passes himself off as a vegetarian, but keeps waking up with blood in his fur.

There is a familiar phrase lurking. 'The very thing I don't want to do, is what I do.' So bloody inevitable. Why not surrender to the process? Give up the mask of virtue, the patently false persona of a man with morals.

And yet that's me as well. I still believe, even though I make a mockery of it from time to time. Stretched between the two horses of love and libido, pulling in opposite directions. And it's cost me everything.

So complicated and so pathetic. So ridiculous and so compromised. Like everyone else I know.

So human.

When Quentin wanders into the kitchen, Claire and John are having a late breakfast. He walks to the refrigerator before stopping, and turning back in wonder.

'Oh god,' he exclaims. 'Don't tell me. I don't want to know any of the sordid details. Claire, my

172

love, I feel jilted — positively jilted. You know you've always been my only true love, and here you are throwing yourself away on some likely lad from the nether side of the world. How could you possibly prefer skimmed milk to cream? There's just no accounting for taste. I'm devastated, absolutely devastated. And pleased for you both, if that's appropriate. I'll probably have to kill myself, but don't you worry about me.'

'We'll send flowers,' says John.

'Not lilies, please. I can't stand lilies. And stop looking at each other, or I swear I'll vomit into the sink.'

Claire succeeds in looking embarrassed and pleased with herself at the same time.

Tasha closes her eyes. It helps her to concentrate on the flow; to see the path through to its conclusion; to regain the sense of the big picture. When she opens them again, the next step is obvious. A small sub-routine she's used before. It flows out through her fingers and takes shape on the screen.

'Have you got a minute, Tasha?'

She turns to find her immediate supervisor, Judith, standing behind her. A fiftyish and formidable woman, Judith has looked out for Tasha from the day she hired her. They share the same instincts for survival, the same practical cynicism.

Tasha follows her back to her office. They sit in the comfortable chairs to one side of the large

> **Constant togetherness is fine — but only for Siamese twins.**
> Victoria Billings

glass desk. The offer of coffee is made and declined.

'This looks serious,' says Tasha, rehearsing the various possibilities.

'I suppose it is in a way. However, it's nothing for you to worry about. In fact it's rather good news, I should imagine.'

Tasha's brow immediately wrinkles in a frown. Good news should always be treated with suspicion; bad news is to be expected.

'We're offering you a promotion, if you'd like it. Slightly less hands-on, more supervision of staff, and another 10K.'

'Doing what, specifically?'

'Doing my job,' says Judith, eyeing Tasha directly.

'Which means?'

'I'm taking some time out. I've been having some tests, and I've been diagnosed with bowel cancer. I'm going into hospital next week for an op. I need time to recuperate, and even if it goes well I'm not sure that I'll come back. So there's an opening, and there was never any question but that it would go to you.'

'Oh shit. Judith, I'm so sorry. I don't know what to say... you must be shattered.'

'It takes more than cancer to rattle an old warhorse like me. The surgeon thinks there's a good chance he'll get it all, but I'm realistic about the odds. It's a bloody nuisance, that's all, because I was supposed to be flying out to see my granddaughter in a few weeks...'

I like to burn my bridges before I come to them.

Leonard Rossiter

Tasha reaches over and takes Judith's hand, gripping it firmly. She has caught the hesitation in Judith's voice, and noticed the wetness of eye. Here, they are no longer employer and employee. They are two strong women, facing into the cold winds, unsure at last that they can keep order by sheer strength of personality. But women together.

It takes her by surprise. Siobhàn is uncharacteristically maudlin. She has been trying to shake it all day, but it clings like a damp blackness to her soul. The cause is obvious, though she has been skirting around it, preferring other possibilities.

Quentin told her on Sunday night. She had noticed them spending more time together but, for some bloody stupid reason, hadn't thought anything of it. In this most open of mysteries, her intuition had failed her completely. It seemed so unlikely, that must be why. She remembers his hard lean body, and the almost tragic softness of Claire. How can these things be?

Not that I have any reason to complain. I spelled it out to him; I took pains to explain that it was just a meeting of our bodies. I've slept with three men since that night. I'm free and he's free. We're grown-ups; we had sex with no complications. So why am I feeling this way? How is it that it's got under my skin?

My life is so fucked up and lonely.

There is a somewhat subdued air to the night as they gather on Friday. They'd lost track of

Every age seems to be accompanied by a sickness so peculiarly its own as to make one wonder if it is not merely a physical manifestation of the inner aberration of the time itself: and cancer certainly, within and without, is our very own.
Laurens van der Post

Claire's Greek Lemon and Rice Soup

4 cups boiling water

4–5 teaspoons powdered chicken stock

1 single breast fillet chicken (skinless)

White pepper to taste

Half cup rice or risotto

2–3 eggs

2 tablespoons lemon juice

Boil 4 cups of water, and when boiling add chicken stock. Stir until well dissolved and add the rice and white pepper. Finely chop the chicken into small cubes. Add to the liquid 10 minutes after adding the rice. When the rice is soft, separate the eggs and put the egg whites in a small bowl. Keep the yolks. Beat the egg whites while adding the lemon juice. As soon as it starts to stiffen, add yolks and beat another 30 seconds. Spoon 2 ladles of liquid into the beaten egg mixture and stir together. Immediately remove the chicken stock from the heat and add the egg mixture, stirring well. Praise Fuzz Kitto as you eat.

whose turn it was to cook, but Claire offered. She'd been altogether more confident and enlivened during the week.

Conversation is jerky and stilted as they make headway into the magnificent soup, a Greek lemon chicken concoction passed on by a friend.

'Oh, for heaven's sake,' sighs Claire eventually. 'Let's talk about it openly. John and I have got closer during this week, and we're spending time together. I know it changes things a bit for how we all get on, but we should be able to work our way through it. We know each other well enough by now not to have to be polite about it all.'

John continues contemplating the wonder of the soup.

'It's none of our business,' says Siobhàn.

Tasha simply starts giggling. She tries to cover it up, but can't help herself, and erupts into full-blown chuckling. 'Sorry,' she chortles as the others stare at her in astonishment.

'It's just that I didn't pick it. John and Claire,' she explains, bursting into another gale of laughter. They all join in, including the initially affronted Claire. Even Siobhàn finds her resentment dissolving in the hilarity.

'What?' asks John as the wave subsides. 'What's so funny?' But he's wiping the corners of his eyes as well.

'Life,' informs Tasha. 'Just life.'

'*L'chaim!*', proposes Siobhàn, 'To Life.'

'What's the frigging topic for tonight, Claire, you silky siren?' Siobhàn inquires.

'Oh no; this is going to come out wrong however I say it,' she wails.

'Say it anyway and we'll promise to misinterpret it,' assures Quentin.

'Commitment,' Claire reveals.

'You're a dead duck, Johnny-boy. Legs up in the water,' Tasha declares, breaking into laughter again.

'Be quiet and give me a chance,' begs Claire. 'It's got nothing to do with John and me. Well… What I'm thinking of is our generation, and what everyone keeps saying about us. That we're slackers, that we have no commitment to anything. My father gave me a lecture about it last week, over my birthday dinner. "You're not striving for anything," he said. "Typical of your whole generation – you've got no goals, no endurance, nothing to aim for." It didn't bother me at the time – Daddy always talks like that – but afterwards I wondered if it were true or not.'

'"Here we are now, entertain us",' pronounces John.

'Sorry?'

'It's just a line, Claire. Go on.'

'When I stopped to think about it, I don't really have any goals in life. I'm not aiming for anything at all. I just live from day to day. I don't have any great purpose or cause to drive me. It doesn't worry me in the least, but I've started wondering if it should. Perhaps I'm missing something important about life.'

Now the whole dizzying and delirious range of sexual possibilities has been boiled down to that one big, boring, bulimic word. RELATIONSHIP.

Julie Burchill

'If you're missing it, darling, then so are the rest of us. If anyone asks me if I have a cause, I assume they're talking about a CD by an Irish band,' Quentin contributes.

'Hang on a minute,' protests Tasha. 'Before you start including the whole cosmos in your own benighted view of reality, I wish to point out that I at least possess a few humble goals, and I'm not ashamed to admit it. I don't buy this whole generational typecasting thing. It's no different from racial prejudice when you come down to it.'

'How so?' asks Siobhàn.

'Ascribing characteristics to a whole generation isn't much different from saying all Dutch people are tight or all Asians are hopeless drivers.'

'I can't fault you on those two maxims,' smirks Quentin.

'Generation X is an invention by the baby boomers,' asserts John. 'They needed someone to be superior to. And they assumed that all young people need a common experience like they had.'

'Still and all,' Siobhàn argues, 'there are certain characteristics about our generation that there's no denying. Generalizations are all right if you take them for what they are. I'd like to get back to what Claire's asking us.'

'Of course we're lacking in commitment,' says Quentin. 'What the firk is there to be committed to? We inherited a ratshit world which had been poisoned, neglected and raped. Our parents fed us all these high-flown ideals while they bought themselves heart attacks chasing after money, or flushed their marriages down the toilet by bonking half the workforce. They left us politicians who couldn't tell the truth to save themselves, teachers who hate their children almost as much as their job, priests who are porking the altar boys in between sermons, and doctors who won't examine until they've had a credit check done. For the first half of our lives we live with the possibility that the whole world will be evaporated because the head of some superpower's feeling paranoid, and then they tell us that it's all been a mistake and we should be the best of friends. We're being screwed over by the multinationals who insist on keeping a lot of us out of work so that the rest of us won't be uppity. If we don't die from AIDS it'll probably be mercury poisoning or BSE. Oh, happy day! Let's all sit down and work out our strategies for the future!'

'So what?' demands Tasha. 'So the world isn't perfect. It wasn't perfect when anyone else was born either. Every generation has something – wars, poverty, disease – something. The difference is that most people, when they face things that are wrong, set about trying to do something to change the world. They don't take their game off into a corner and start crying about it. I'm with Claire's father on this one – that self-pitying crap doesn't wash for one minute. It's self-indulgent, that's what it is.'

> **Choose us. Choose life. Choose mortgage payments; choose washing machines; choose cars; choose sitting oan a couch watching mind-numbing and spirit-crushing game shows... Well, ah choose no tae choose life.**
> Irvine Welsh

'Jeez, you sound like my mother,' groans Quentin. 'I can't believe this crap. Where have you been all your life? We don't plan and we don't dream and we don't participate because we don't have any *hope*. We've got no faith in the future. And before you tell me to get some while I'm having a haircut, it's not a choice that we don't have hope. It's not like we all sat around and thought, "What are we going to do in our generation? I know, let's do despair – that hasn't been done for a while." We just got born into the world when the sun was going down, and it's dark. No good telling a lame man to dance.'

'Bollocks,' retorts Tasha. 'You're only lame because you've never tried to walk.'

'For me,' suggests John, 'there has to be something that I can commit myself to. I've got to believe that it's worthwhile making an effort, and that if I do put some energy in, it's going to make a difference in the end. I guess I do struggle with commitment to anything significant, and it's probably because I don't believe that anything I do will make a difference. Political power is too entrenched, business is too corrupt, education is too reductionist, and religion is too detached. The only sphere where I feel I can make any sort of contribution is in myself and among my friends.'

'What about your social work?' asks Claire. 'Don't you make a difference there?'

'Hah! There's nothing guaranteed to make you more cynical than a few months doing social work.

I don't consider myself a pessimist at all. I think of a pessimist as someone who is waiting for it to rain. And I feel completely soaked to the skin.

Leonard Cohen

People are locked into these negative cycles that totally consume them. You think you're helping someone to break out, and a few months later they're back the same as they ever were, if not worse off. Human beings are essentially tragic.'

'So why do you do it?' Claire persists.

'I've got nothing else to do. It earns a living, and I don't feel like I'm selling my soul in order to get it. To be honest, I do it because I'm just as helpless as they are, except I know it and most of them don't. It's a way of being a friend and getting paid for it.'

'Bunch of non-productive bludgers, as far as I'm concerned,' scowls Tasha.

'That's one way of describing friendship,' murmurs John.

'I think,' offers Siobhàn, 'that commitment's highly overrated.'

'Explain,' demands Quentin.

'Commitment's an invitation to get hurt, isn't it, now? There's a story from the old country about two fortified castles which were close to each other. The people got friendly, and they decided to dig a tunnel between the two places. It seemed to be a way to keep in touch without exposing themselves to danger outside the walls. But what happened was that a band of pillagers took one of the castles by night, found the tunnel, and crept through it and murdered all the inhabitants of the second one as well. They would have been safer without the tunnel, you see.'

> Hope? I have none and furthermore I condemn it with everything in my power... I don't believe in it. I believe only in my own vitality.
>
> Pier Paolo Pasolini

'So we're better off staying isolated from each other?' asks Quentin incredulously.

'It's all right to get close now and again; just don't ask me to dig tunnels under the walls, that's all.'

'I don't know if it's possible to love without making yourself vulnerable,' Claire says softly.

'Then don't love. Love's a Trojan horse, and we all know that story. Look, when I was ten years old, we had a dog. He was a bit of a mongrel called Blackie. I had the job of feeding him and the two of us got close. It was a big family, and you could easily get lost in it. So I used to wander off on my own with Blackie, and tell him all my secrets. Come to think of it, he was the best listener I've ever come across. I loved that dog – that's the mistake I made, see? I let my defences down. He would always sleep beside my bed, and if I woke up in the night I could reach down and touch him, and he'd lick my hand. The inevitable happened. I was away at school, so I didn't find out till I got home. He'd chased a cat across the road and been hit by a truck. There were scones cooking when I came in. I've always hated scones since. I was inconsolable. I cried all night, and for most of the week after. Nothing has ever got to me in quite that way since Blackie. I learned something then; learned to keep some of me back, whatever I was giving.'

'I'm not sure it works, that's the problem,' responds Claire.

'It's worked all right for me,' insists Siobhàn.

'What you're trying to protect yourself against is being hurt. And you can do that by withdrawing; refusing to expose yourself to danger. But then you just find pain of a different sort – the pain of isolation, the pain of loneliness.'

Siobhàn's face is set resolutely in defiance.

'I don't think you can hold back from loving just because of the risks,' continues Claire. 'Otherwise you might become incapable of loving, and then you wouldn't be human. That's what worries me about the fear of commitment. Maybe it's an attempt to avoid the risks of living fully, to withdraw into ourselves so that we don't get hurt.'

'And what, precisely, is wrong with that?' inquires Tasha. 'Self-protection seems perfectly legitimate to me.'

'But it's ultimately selfish, isn't it?' Claire counters. 'You're looking after yourself by separating from others, whereas risking your life for the sake of someone else is what love is all about.'

'Unless a grain of wheat falls into the ground and dies, it abides alone,' John contributes.

'You what?' demands Tasha. 'Come again?'

'Unless a grain of wheat falls into the ground and dies, it abides alone.'

'That's good,' admits Tasha. 'I might get you to write that down for me after.'

'It's not original,' John confesses.

··········

I think there was a trade-off somewhere along the line. I think the price we paid for our golden life was an inability to fully believe in love; instead we gained an irony that scorched everything it touched.

Douglas Coupland

I tell you, unless a grain of wheat falls into the earth and dies, it remains just a single grain; but if it dies, it bears much fruit.

Jesus

'Here's a scenario,' proffers Quentin, reluctantly setting aside the lasagne. 'A couple meet, they fall in love. They do everything the right way: a formal engagement, a big party, all that sort of thing. The wedding is huge and white, and in the presence of their families and friends they promise each other undying love. In fact they promise to stay together until they die. For the first bit everything goes swimmingly, but gradually the passion begins to cool. She starts noticing his annoying habits, and begins a crusade to correct them. He spends more and more time away from home, and begins to resent her. They have children, and this provides a welcome distraction. Eventually the children turn into teenagers and do their normal teenage thing.

'This makes life tense around home. The parents turn on each other in their frustration. She meets a man at the opera. He's older, suave, East European and gloriously unattached. Though she doesn't mean to, she ends up in bed with him. It begins a long cycle of betrayal and deceit. In the meantime, her husband has been bonking one of the supervisors from the office next door to his. When she gives him the heave-ho, he moves on to one of his own junior staff who thinks it might help with a promotion. At home, the couple falls into a welcome pattern of cohabitation without communication. They suspect each other, and one night it all comes out in an explosion of recrimination. When it all settles down, they decide to stay together for the

184

sake of the children. At their silver wedding, there are a lot of speeches about their remarkable achievement of preserving a commitment for twenty-five years.

'Another couple meets at the same time as our first lot. This pair is all over the place. They don't know whether they love each other or not. Their relationship swings wildly between spectacular arguments and intense passion. They end up moving in together, though they are careful to remind each other not to expect anything out of it. Both of them are vibrant creative people. At times they hardly see each other because they are involved in different social scenes. But when they get together they have a lot to talk about. Then she becomes pregnant. He suspects it's an attempt to tie him down and tells her so. She promptly moves out, but they can't live without each other, and so the separation only lasts a couple of weeks.

'After the baby is born, there is pressure on them from family members to get married. They refuse. After all, they explain, we don't know if we'll still be together in a year from now. We're just taking things day by day. Well, the days go by. The child grows up. Despite several good offers, they remain faithful to one another. Always at the last minute, they can't bear the thought of hurting their partner. The relationship remains volatile, and they pride themselves on not being married. But one day they wake up and discover that twenty-five years have gone by since the day they moved in together.

The guarantee of freedom is freedom. Michel Foucault

'So, the question is, which couple is committed?'

'That's all a bit stereotypical, isn't it?' Claire protests.

'The first couple is my parents. The other is my uncle and his partner, on my mother's side.'

'Oh,' says Claire.

'So what are you saying?' asks Tasha. 'That it's better to have no commitment at all than to try and to fail?'

'As may have been said on previous occasions, I'm not saying anything – I'm just telling a story. But if you want my opinion, yes; it's better not to promise things which you have no knowing you can keep, than to speak empty words. I feel like my feet have been bleeding all my life from walking over the shards of other people's promises.'

'So you're going to preserve your purity by promising nothing?'

'I'm just doing my best to be honest and keep my head down,' sighs Quentin. 'I imagine that if I can refrain from adding to the problem, I will have made a contribution to humanity.'

'Risk nothing, gain nothing,' Tasha sneers.

'How about the idea that commitment expands your capacity?' asks John tentatively. 'Sometimes you need to test yourself against possibilities that you're unsure you can live up to. Like this one time I went bungee jumping. I told everyone I was going to do it, but when I got out on the platform on the bridge and looked down, I was terrified. My brain was absolutely scrambled. If I hadn't had friends watching I would have backed down. But there were only two choices — to jump or not to jump. In the end I somehow launched myself, and after the first few seconds, it was one of the most exhilarating experiences of my life. Anything could have gone wrong — a couple of people have died there — but it turned out to be all right. If I'd backed out because of the danger, I never would've had the experience. I've often thought about that when I've been at weddings.'

'Yeah, except the comparison with weddings would be that about fifty per cent of the punters died on the rocks below, and thirty per cent of the rest of them were crippled for life,' objects Quentin.

'Fair enough,' admits John. 'But I still think the point's valid. If you only commit yourself to things you know you're capable of, it's not going to stretch you much, is it?'

'When it comes to bungee jumping, I'm quite happy to remain unstretched,' Quentin responds.

> Some people are born slack — others have slackness thrust upon them.
> Will Self

'But what about other sorts of commitments, apart from relationships?' Claire resumes. 'Here we are, the five of us, all at the age where we've got energy and time, and what is any of us doing to change the world in which we live?'

'I tidied the lounge last Saturday,' ventures Siobhàn.

'And I once owned up when I got too much change at the newsagent's,' claims Quentin.

'Precisely,' Claire rebukes. 'We've rather given up on the world, haven't we?'

'It's too bloody hopeless, Claire,' argues Quentin. 'I'd rather bang my head against a brick wall, and I'd probably have more effect. The world's got beyond our changing – I don't honestly believe that there's anything I could do that would make a blind bit of a difference. I could go and set fire to myself in Trafalgar Square like one of those Buddhist monks, but after they'd put the fire out, everyone would go on their own way. It's got to the stage where if the world's going to change, it's going to have to change itself. I'm not going to take responsibility for it.'

'So what, then?' Tasha demands. 'You stick your head up your bum, and hope it'll all go away? I can't see what right you've got to complain if you're not doing anything to change the way things are.'

'I do what's in me to do,' he counters.

'And what's that?'

'I tell stories.'

'We *are* doing something,' Siobhàn insists.

'And what would that be, apart from eating good food and drinking good wine?' asks John.

'We're talking. Getting to know each other a little. And discussing some interesting stuff. I'm getting to like these Friday nights, and it's got me

188

thinking about all sorts of things. So let's not be too down on ourselves, yeah?'

'Right enough,' agrees John. 'Though I keep feeling we're on the verge of something that we never quite reach.'

'What've you got in mind?' asks Claire.

'I don't know what it is. All I can say is that every now and again we get close to it, and then we bounce off into some new issue. Maybe it's a matter of building up trust in each other, or maybe it's me hoping for something more than's realistic. But I just have the feeling that we're avoiding the *really* deep stuff. It'll happen if it's meant to.'

'And in the meantime, let them eat cake,' suggests Claire. 'Specifically, an orange and cointreau cake. Any takers?'

Sharing food with another human being is an intimate act that should not be indulged in lightly.
M.F.K. Fisher

Chapter Ten

She's reading the paper when he ambles in. The fact that it's John makes her groan inwardly. There must be some law against being garrulous before noon.

'Morning, Tasha,' he grins. He shapes to whistle while making his coffee, but glances at Tasha and decides against it. Instead he beats a short rhythm with the knife on a plate.

'John,' she begins, laying aside the news in defeat, 'have you ever considered taking sedatives? Or sleeping pills? Just a little something to take the manic edge off your unbounded exuberance?'

'Sorry,' John concedes. 'Or almost sorry. Don't you feel the life surging in your veins when you wake? The unstained day stretching out before you, full of hope and wonder?'

Hope is the feeling you have that the feeling you have isn't permanent.

Jean Kerr

'I don't feel anything for at least two hours. I'm speaking to you through a fog of indifference. It won't clear until the sun burns it off some time from now. I've not become aware of the day yet, and so I have no opinion as to what it may hold. But at this early stage, I'd say it's probably got off to a poor start.'

'Bloody English,' mutters John.

'What's that?'

'Nothing.'

A sort of silence descends temporarily, punctuated only by John's enthusiastic munching of toast. He tries unsuccessfully to read headlines from the paper which Tasha has folded defiantly under her elbow.

'John,' she ventures a little tentatively. 'Now you've spoiled my morning, there's something you might be able to do for me.'

'Shoot,' invites John, raising his eyebrows.

'You know how you've said that you say prayers or something?'

'I pray rather than say, but yes.'

'It's just that I've got this friend at work, Judith, and she's having an operation for bowel cancer tomorrow. I wondered if you might pray for her?'

'I'd be glad to, Tasha. You could pray for her yourself, if you wanted to. Just to keep me company.'

'Hah!' she dismisses.

If you talk to God, you are praying; if God talks to you, you have schizophrenia.

Thomas Szasz

Siobhàn pauses in the midst of the project for self-examination. There's a sadness below the surface like a womb full of rocks. She stops to recall where it comes from.

Tony had rung to tell her. She didn't know what to say in response. William had tried to kill himself. Driven his car off into the country. Found a deserted spot and put a hose on the exhaust pipe. Why is it always men that do that? Women would never use a *car* to do themselves in. So mechanical and unemotional; so lacking in imagination.

Someone had driven past and hauled him out.

No one is promiscuous in his way of dying. A man who has decided to hang himself will never jump in front of a train.

Alvarez

Now he was in hospital, and they suspected brain damage. Bastard! How dare he do this to me; make me feel like this?

Was it only a week ago she'd been in his bed? Waking early and noting the pathetic collection of toy cars in a stand on the wall. And the picture on the dresser — I'd lay odds it's his mother. He was cloyingly tender and romantic, treating her like a virgin on a honeymoon. When what she'd wanted was roughness, ravishing. She needed that night to be nailed to the wall, to feel pain and loving and not tell the difference.

I frightened him, I think. Came on a little strong; pushed him further than he'd ever been. Made him feel dirty for liking it so much. I was angry with him afterwards. Angry that he wanted me but didn't want *me*. He was after some image of his virtuous mother that he put on me. And he screwed up his face when I was swearing, as if I'd hit him.

Maybe that's why I was so cruel to him on the phone afterwards. I wanted to hurt him; wanted to ruin his smarmy self-confidence. Did I say something about hoping for more from the night? I think I did.

And now the bastard wants to get the last word. Wants me to feel guilty because he's a spineless mummy's boy, and can't hack it in the fast lane. Well, I refuse.

Except that I do. Feel guilty.

He's meeting a friend in town, so Quentin catches the bus in with Claire. It's an adventure

True guilt is guilt at the obligation one owes to oneself to be oneself. False guilt is guilt felt at not being what other people feel one ought to be or assume that one is.

R.D. Laing

for him, pretending to be a commuter like all the others. With a job to go to.

Claire is so refined in the midst of all this commerce and banality. Too good for the bus, he thinks.

'How are you doing, my darling?' he asks her. 'Tell Uncle Quentin how it's all going.'

She surfaces from that private world which is her home. Her face lights in a smile.

'I'm better than I've been for a long time, Quentin. I'm very happy.'

'Are you, chook? That's wonderful. I'm truly pleased for you. Even though I'm devastated that you should choose that wild colonial boy over a superior specimen such as my good self. You know I've always been in love with you, don't you?'

'Oh Quentin. I don't know that you've ever been in love with anyone. You're in love with the idea of love.'

'You cut me to the quick, my dear. Truth, I always say, should be left to the vulgar and unimaginative. There's no need to be quite so brutally *honest*. If it weren't for the fact I adore you, I might be mortally offended.'

Claire looks at him and giggles, and then kisses him on the cheek.

'You're a good friend, Quentin. Thanks for being around.'

'There's my epitaph. Quentin died abandoned and alone, but he was a good friend. May his bones rest in splendour, and his heart in solitude.'

Fantasy love is much better than reality love. Never doing it is very exciting.
Andy Warhol

'You do talk a lot of nonsense.'

'It's what I do, Claire; it's what I do.'

Tasha surprises them all. Not only has she volunteered to cook, but the result appears quite passable. They begin with calamari accompanied by a spicy sauce. Though she dismisses the compliments, she looks well pleased with herself.

'The sauce is out of a bottle,' she informs them.

'It's delicious, Tasha,' says Siobhàn. 'You're letting the side down here – raising the standards for all of us.'

'I only volunteered because I wanted to choose the topic for tonight.'

'Must be something burning on your heart,' suggests Quentin.

'Death,' suggests Tasha.

'Is that a curse or the topic?' asks Quentin.

'It's what we're going to talk about,' Tasha insists.

'I guess I've been thinking about it because of this woman at work who's got cancer. She's only middle-aged really. A strong competent woman, who knows where she's going and how to get there. She's made it in a male-dominated industry by being able to play hardball with the best of them. I've never seen her fearful of anything before, except now. Suddenly life has a potential full stop to it, and it's nothing that's within her ability to control. And I don't know what the hell

The difference between sex and death is that with death you can do it alone and no one is going to make fun of you.

Woody Allen

to say to her. She's a lot like me, Judith. Maybe that's why it's got me so rattled.'

'The long shadow of mortality,' suggests John.

'I'm not sure that I like to talk about death,' says Siobhàn. 'It'll be coming soon enough. "You'll be calling it out of the night," my Da used to say, "and then there's no knowing who it'll come to visit." We're young enough to ignore it, aren't we?'

'It's part of life,' argues John. 'You can't talk about life without talking about death. It's as natural as breathing.'

'Or the lack of it,' quips Quentin.

'In our house we never mentioned death,' reveals Claire. 'It was always someone "passing away" or a neighbour "losing her husband". The few times I went to funerals I wondered what was in the shiny box, because my parents would never talk about it. I still find it a bit creepy, but I think it's good to talk about it.'

'Ah, go on then,' allows Siobhàn. 'Maybe I've had my close encounter for this week anyway.'

> We are all of us resigned to death: it's life we aren't resigned to.
>
> Graham Greene

'I guess you try to avoid it as much as you can,' continues Tasha. 'It's something that happens to other people. And then it comes close to you and you remember that one day, however far off it may be, it's coming for you as well. I see myself in Judith, and the fact that she's scared has made me wonder if I'd be ready for it.'

'You shouldn't ever be ready for it,' protests Quentin. 'To accept death is to give up on life. Do not go gentle into that good night, and all that.'

'Didn't stop him dying young, though, did it?' offers John.

'Who?' asks Claire.

'Dylan Thomas,' provides Quentin. 'I wasn't suggesting you can avoid death; just that you shouldn't lie down and let it tramp all over you. Being alive is a struggle against death, and if you let your guard down for a minute, it'll claim you.'

'Your gran, was she ready to die?' inquires John.

'In a way, she was. But she was old — it was inevitable. Maybe by that stage you get so tired that you can't fight any more. Death comes and tidies you away like a bit of old dust on the floor.'

'God, I'm not ready for it, I don't mind admitting,' confesses Siobhàn. 'I've got too much living to do.'

'I think death concentrates life,' muses John.

'Cancels it more like,' retorts Siobhàn. 'What d'you mean, concentrates it?'

'If you live like you're never going to die, pretending it'll never happen, then you procrastinate and hold back. There'll always be another day, you tell yourself, or another person. But if you know that death is the horizon we're all working against, then you make each day count, and you live to the max. Look what happens to people when they get told they've only got a certain amount of time left. They make sure that they sort out their relationships, and they savour every experience that's left for them to enjoy.'

'What's everyone's first experience of death?' Tasha asks.

··········

'When I was at school,' begins John, 'there was a guy named John Steel who played the same position as me in rugby. We were both on the side of the scrum. He was better than me, and so he ended up always a team ahead of me. Sometimes I'd go and watch him play – he was really good, and I figured I could learn from him. We got on pretty well, even though in a sense we were rivals. By our last year in school, he was a star in the first fifteen, and I was grinding away in the second fifteen.

'Even though I liked John, I was envious of the natural skills he had, and how popular it made him.

'He was into blues music. We'd swap music, and sometimes see each other at a blues club in town called Sweetheart. We were probably the youngest people there. John would always stop and chat, though there was usually some girl hanging off his arm or sizing him up from a distance. One lunchtime, he invited a few of us round to his house, which was just near the school. He had this great track he wanted to play for us. It was the first time I'd ever heard John Mayall's 'Room to Move', and it blew my socks off. We listened to it a few times through, and then he wound the volume up full tit, and we just all danced around the room, loving it.

'John was totally caught up in it. He was a great dancer, and I have this wonderful picture of him

How long after you are gone will ripples remain as evidence that you were cast into the pool of life?
Grant M. Bright

in my mind, hair flying everywhere, eyes closed, a huge grin on his face, and dancing his heart out. Two weeks later he was playing a game of rugby, and got caught at the bottom of a ruck. He came off the field, complaining of a sore head. It didn't seem that bad. He died in his sleep that night. At home in his bed. He just expired, and was no more. It seemed incredible that anyone with that much life and vitality could up and stop on us. But that was it; dead as dead could be. I still have trouble believing he's gone.'

'In Ireland, death's like a cousin, always coming round to visit. I grew up with corpses in the sitting room,' recalls Siobhàn. 'So it's hard to remember my first encounter. But the one that sticks in my mind is my Uncle Kevin. He was an old souse, a whiskey drinker of wide repute. I remember the way his cheeks were always red and lumpy with broken blood vessels. But he was a great storyteller, was Kevin, and he loved children. So whenever we went to visit him, he'd sit us down and then start off on some fantastic tale or other. It was magic, listening to him. We'd be transported off into some wonderful world which he'd be making for us.

'"Kevin, stop your blarney and give the young ones a rest," his wife would say. But he'd take no notice of her. Sometimes he'd lift one cheek of his vast bum and fart loudly, and we'd all be giggling. "Now who did that?" he'd say, looking up as if it were an angel had done it. I used to love to go and

> When I die I want to decompose in a barrel of porter and have it served in all the pubs in Dublin.
>
> J.P. Donleavy

visit him, but my mother wasn't too keen on it. "He's just a drunken fool," she'd say, but he was her favourite brother just the same. She was keening something awful when he died, and we had the wake at our place.

I don't know what he died of. Too much blood in his alcohol stream, my father suggested. He was propped up in an armchair, before they put him in the coffin. I came out at night, because I wanted to keep him company. There was my mother, sitting beside him and holding his hand and crying. First off, she was angry at me for getting out of bed, and then she called me back to come and sit with her. I sat on the floor at his feet, and I expected any minute he'd start telling us a story. But he never did. He just sat there without farting, and not saying a word. I was disappointed, but it wasn't scary in the least. I was happy to let them bury him after that.'

'My story's dull by comparison,' ventures Claire. 'I honestly think my first brush with death was my goldfish, Kissy. She was my first ever pet, when I was about four years old. I got to help buy her, and to choose the bowl. And when they'd put her in a plastic bag to bring home, I nursed her in the front of the car with more devotion than most mothers. Decorating the bowl was such fun, and I sacrificed a couple of my small plastic dolls to the deep. Only Daddy had to weight them down with something to make them stay there. Their hair used to waft

Fish die belly upward, and rise to the surface. It's their way of falling.
André Gide

around in the water, and sometimes Kissy would seem to smooch them.

'And then one morning I got up, and called Mummy to see because Kissy was swimming funny. She was on top of the water. I thought perhaps she was learning to float. Even after I was told she was dead, I didn't believe it. I kept trying to push her along in the water, to get her started. Mummy told me we'd have to get rid of her. When I heard she was going to flush Kissy down the toilet, I put up such a fuss that she decided to bury her in the garden. We made a coffin out of an old soap box and cotton wool, and we laid her in a hole in the ground, alongside the two dolls. In springtime, I often went out to check the ground, in case Kissy had sprouted into a fish plant. I refused to have another goldfish, in case the same thing happened.'

A dead atheist is someone who is all dressed up with no place to go.
James Duffecy

'My father's death was always with us, from the first times I can remember,' contributes Tasha. 'It didn't seem like something which had *happened*; more like the country we had come from. I don't think I had any idea of what death actually was, apart from the fact that it was something dark and nasty which had robbed us all of the only chance at happiness that we had had. When my mother got drunk, she would curse my father and death and God all in the same breath. She hated the fact that he'd died, and blamed him for it, as if he'd upped and left her, which I suppose he had in a way.

'The first funeral I remember was for some friend of my mother's. I didn't know the person who'd died, but Mum dressed me up in my best clothes, complete with white gloves, and dragged me along. It was in a crematorium chapel. I can't recall anything of what was said. There was shiny brown wood and a lot of droning voices, and from time to time the choking sound of someone sobbing. The most interesting part was the end, when everyone was standing and a tall man in a black suit pressed a button. There was a whirring noise, and then the coffin slid away on a conveyor belt, through some curtains. It seemed like a sort of magic trick to me at the time.

'I was fascinated with where it had gone. I asked my mother, when we'd got outside. She said it'd gone to be burned up. I thought that was revolting. Burning was what we did with our paper rubbish, and it didn't seem right to do that with people. Somehow I got it all mixed up with ideas about hell, and assumed that everyone who died was being whisked away on conveyor belts to be tortured in the flames. I made up my mind it was never going to happen to me, even if it meant I had to make sure I didn't die. I've always been slightly repulsed by funerals, ever since. I'll do anything I can to avoid them.'

Dying is the most embarrassing thing that can ever happen to you, because someone's got to take care of all your details.
Andy Warhol

'I love funerals,' responds Quentin. 'They're much more fun than weddings. I love watching the way that people react when they're in the presence of death — it brings out the best and

worst in people. My Gran dying was the first
encounter I had with the black lady, and I've told
you all about that. But then the funeral – in many
ways that was the best part of the whole story.
The priest who was taking it was a doddering old
fool who kept getting Gran's name wrong.
Whenever he came to the bit in the text with a
blank spot to put in the name of the deceased,
he'd pause, look around desperately to try to find
it in his notes, and then mumble something which
he hoped sounded approximately right.

'My father was furious. After the service he
marched up to the priest and began to tear strips
off him. He told him he was a bloody poor
advertisement for Christianity, and that if that
was the sort of representative God had on earth,
then it wasn't surprising that no one believed in
God anymore. The priest was a little stunned by
the ferocity of the attack, but then he regained his
confidence and began to give back as good as he
was getting. He accused my father of being a
heathen, and said he was setting a jolly poor
example to his family if he didn't go to church.
The world was going to the dogs, he said, all
because of people like my father who didn't have
the moral courage to stand against the tide.

'I thought my father was going to punch him. I
was standing next to him, and I could see how
tightly his fists were balled. But somehow he
restrained himself. He just marched off, turning
round to shout at the priest that he was a leech
feeding on public sorrow, and should be struck off

the roll or whatever the appropriate term was. My mother was mortified, so to speak, and refused to talk in the car all the way to the graveside. I wondered if my father would push the priest into the grave along with the coffin, and cover them both over, but he seemed to have calmed down by then. Poor old Gran was quite forgotten in the furore over her funeral. We children thought it was marvellous, of course. Great entertainment.'

'I'm scared shitless by death, I don't mind admitting it,' says Tasha. 'I can't stand the thought of it happening to me. I must be some egotist, but I just can't bring myself to imagine not being around. It seems wrong somehow. And as for Siobhàn having a dead body hanging around in the lounge – yuck. I'd have to move out; I couldn't stand it.'

'There's nothing wrong with bodies,' asserts Siobhàn. 'They're just empty people.'

'I had a cousin who was an undertaker,' recalls Quentin. 'A couple of years ago I asked him to show me round his workplace. I thought it would be good experience as a writer. Fascinating stuff. He had a client on the premises that he was doing up for the funeral. You've no idea how hard it is to dress a dead person. Their limbs don't bend, and they get bloody heavy. I watched him doing the embalming – they pump all the blood out and replace it with some preservative stuff.'

'That's disgusting,' moans Tasha.

'And to stop the mouth flopping open, they

I'm not afraid to die, I just don't want to be there when it happens.
Woody Allen

stitch the bottom of the jaw to the roof of the mouth; strange but true.'

'I warn you, I'm going to belt you if you don't shut up,' Tasha growls.

'But honestly, Tash, it's not that frightening once you get used to it. A body's like a human-size rubber suit which no one is using any more. There's no way you could mistake it for a real person.'

'There's something goes out of a person when they die,' agrees Siobhàn. 'You can see them change.'

'Like what?' asks Claire. 'A soul?'

'Whatever you want to call it; a soul, life-force, personality. Something changes, and even though the body is sort of familiar, it's not the person anymore.'

'That's the big one, isn't it?' reflects John. 'What happens after death? What becomes of us?'

There is a moment's silence. They pause to eat. The main course is Beef Stroganoff on a bed of rice. From a packet, Tasha had been quick to inform them.

'Nothing,' Tasha pronounces. 'That's what's so horrid about it. It's just a big black full stop. You finish, come to an end, cease to exist. Your body and brain and everything that's you breaks down into the bits that it's made of. Death is the end of every chance you ever had, so if you haven't had a good time before then, it's too late.'

'No wonder you're scared of dying, if that's what you believe,' suggests Claire.

'I'm a realist. I believe in what I see, not in fairy tales.'

'What about all those people who've had near-death experiences?' counters Siobhàn. 'Every one of them reports pretty much the same thing. They journey through a long tunnel, and then they emerge into a fantastic light, where they're met by people they love. And then they discover their time isn't up yet, and they're called back to their bodies. All of them, without fail, lose their fear of death.'

'And doctors have already pointed out that something like that experience might be what is generated by the brain being deprived of oxygen. It doesn't prove anything.'

'I prefer it to the thought of simply rotting in the ground,' retorts Siobhàn. 'If I thought there was nothing after death I'd top myself now and get the waiting over with.'

'Would you though?' Tasha interrogates. 'There's something about life that's pretty damned attractive. It takes a hell of a lot for someone to give up on it altogether.'

And all Siobhàn can think of is William, lying alone in a hospital bed.

'What's your alternative to nothingness, Siobhàn?' asks John.

'Well, it could be anything, couldn't it, now? Reincarnation, wandering as a spirit, some sort of afterlife? I'm an agnostic when it comes to the details, but I'm convinced there's

> Death is an endless night so awful to contemplate that it can make us love life and value it with such passion that it may be the ultimate cause of all joy and all art.
>
> Paul Theroux

something. There's too much I've seen and experienced to believe that death cancels out life. Life is too powerful to put an end to just like that. Besides which, it would be a terrible bloody waste, wouldn't it? All the complexity of a human person coming to nothing – I can't believe that.'

'I believe in heaven,' says Claire quietly.

'Before or after death?' inquires Quentin.

'After, silly. I'm a traditionalist, I suppose. I think we make our choices in this one life, and death resolves them.'

'Quick quiz; which is the more attractive? Eternity sitting in pristine glory being good and smiling, or the prospect of everlasting torment in the fires of hell? You mean there's no third option? No, sorry, you've taken too long. It's off to heaven with you. No, no, anything but that.'

'Want to hear a good heaven story?' asks John.

'Always,' encourages Siobhàn.

'It's the end of the world, and God has gathered everyone who ever lived in heaven. They're all assembled there in front of the throne, ready for the judgment. "Here's what we're going to do," says God. "The archangel Gabriel here is going to read out the ten commandments, one by one. Everyone who's kept the commandments can stay, but those who've broken them will have to depart into outer darkness, I'm afraid." So it starts; Gabriel reads the first commandment, and a large number of the crowd are ushered off into the distance. The reading proceeds with the

There will be sex after death; we just won't be able to feel it.

Lily Tomlin

commandments one after another, each time with a pause for people to leave.

'After the one about adultery has been read, God looks up. There's a fairly small crowd left. Those remaining are thin-lipped ascetic types, with stern brows and a righteous gleaming in their eyes. God pauses and contemplates the prospect of spending eternity with this lot. "All right," he cries out. "Everyone come back. I've changed my mind."'

'But getting back to dying,' Tasha insists, 'it doesn't matter what any of us believes, because none of us has been there and no one's come back to tell us what happens. And the fact is that all of us are going to have to face it, without knowing what the outcome is.'

'I'm with you on that one,' concedes John. 'No matter what any of us think, we all walk into the dark alone.'

'I've been with a few people now when they've died,' says Siobhàn. 'It's different every time. Some of the old ones seem to welcome it, as if they're finally being allowed to get to sleep after someone's been keeping them awake too long. But I had an auntie dying of cancer who fought it all the way. She was out of it on morphine by the time the end came, but her face was still locked in a grimace. That was no easy death.'

'How do you let go of something you've got used to holding onto?' wonders Tasha.

'"Rage, rage, against the dying of the light";

Every man must do two things alone; he must do his own believing and his own dying.
Martin Luther

that's my philosophy,' explains Quentin. 'As soon as you give in, you've begun to die already.'

'It's not like you're going to avoid it, though, is it?' responds John. 'I think it's all about accepting the fact that life ends in death. Once you've taken that on board, it can either take away all meaning from life and make it futile, or else it can make you value and appreciate every experience you have, every breath you draw. I can't see that you have to fight death in order to love life. Seems to me the people who have it most together are those who are ready to face death whenever it comes, but who throw themselves into life with a passion.'

'I'm not ready for death,' admits Tasha.

'I don't suppose I am either, truth be told,' says John. 'I accept the idea of dying, but I'm not sure about the reality. A friend of mine used to say that the task of life is to learn how to die. I've got a long way to go.'

'I sometimes dream,' recounts Quentin, 'that I'm being buried alive. I'm in a coffin, and I can hear the sound of the clay banging on the lid. I try to move; to call out and tell people that I'm alive, but I realize that I can't move a muscle. And then it occurs to me that perhaps I am dead. It's the most terrifying of all my dreams. I wake up rigid with fear.'

'I've had that dream!' exclaims Tasha.

'Me too!' laughs Siobhàn. 'D'you think it's a repeat?'

'Why does everyone have to wear black to funerals?' asks Claire. 'Black's so unflattering on

How you die is the most important thing you ever do. It's the exit, the final scene of the glorious epic of your life. It's the third act and, you know, everything builds up to the third act.
Timothy Leary

While I thought that I was learning how to live, I have been learning how to die.
Leonardo da Vinci

me. Surely there must be other colours that people could wear?'

For a long time afterwards John wondered how it happened. He might have had too much to drink. The conversation was intriguing, and he was completely at ease and disarmed. But even so, that didn't explain it.

'I heard a story,' starts Quentin, 'about a minister who was presiding over a burial in Australia. Apparently the ground was really sandy, and as he was standing there pronouncing a blessing, the side of the grave collapsed and he landed there on top of the coffin, cursing to the heavens.'

'That's nothing,' rejoins John, 'There was this one time in Taranaki when I was doing the committal, and the water table in the district was really...'

'Hang on,' jumps in Tasha. 'What'd you say?'

'What?'

'You said you were doing the committal. Didn't he?' Tasha looks to the others for support.

'Oh shit,' says John.

At the moment of death, I hope to be surprised.
Ivan Illich

Chapter Eleven

It's not the best of times for one of his blank spots, but he has no control over them. A lacuna of the spirit; a menopause of the imagination. Retreating into ovarian oblivion, where every sense is muffled.

But several sets of eyes are stapling him to the wall in expectation. As he breaks the surface, he's aware that his face is smiling, stupidly.

'I was a priest,' he says simply.

'Holy Mary, Mother of God,' invokes Siobhàn.

'I knew it!' claims Quentin.

'What do you mean?' asks Claire.

Tasha merely narrows her eyes in fresh cynicism. When in doubt, doubt.

'A Catholic priest,' adds John, as if this aids understanding.

'But how could you be?' demands Claire, baffled.

'You do your training, you get priested, and bingo, you're a priest,' he explains.

'But you're not old enough,' she insists. 'You can't have been doing it for very long?'

'A bit more than a year.'

'Tell, tell,' demands Siobhàn. 'From the beginning.'

'Absolutely,' agrees Quentin.

'It was always on the horizon. Priests were the heroes of the faith, and it was understood in the

The priesthood in many ways is the ultimate closet in Western civilization...

John Spong

He was of the faith chiefly in the sense that the church he currently did not attend was Catholic.

Kingsley Amis

family that our parents wanted at least one of us to have a religious vocation. I used to watch the face of the priest during the prayer of consecration, and I wanted to know what it felt like. There was some sort of mystery there, some sort of treading on the edges of eternity. It was more intriguing to me than any of the wonders of scientific discovery. Looking back on it now, I'd say there was always a hunger to be involved. And then at confirmation, the Bishop handed out medals to each of us. One of them had a cross engraved on the reverse side, and I ended up getting it. It was decided at random, as far as I know; I took it as a sign. I never told anyone; I just kept it to myself.

'I don't think my parents ever imagined it would be me who took up the calling. I was always getting into trouble for one thing or another. Fighting with other kids, or stealing money out of milk bottles to buy smokes with. A couple of times we had family conferences with me, my parents and the priest, to try to work out "what could be done with him". Even though I secretly wanted to be a priest, I was determined I would never be a goody-goody. Our priest was old, in his last parish. He was a canny old bloke, and I'm sure he picked up something of what was going on within me. He kept me back after one of the parental inquisitions, and talked to me for a bit. "John," he said to me, "whatever God decides for you will come to be. There's no need to fight for it or fight against it." After that I relaxed a lot.

To all things clergic,
I am allergic.
Alexander Woollcott

'There was never any blinding light or anything. Just a growing fascination with life and God and people and a hunch that what happened in the Mass had something important to do with it all. And to be honest, it seemed kind of easy to slip into the seminary without thinking about what else I might want to do in life. The funny thing is that on the night before I left, my father took me down to the pub and tried to talk me out of it. Well, not so much talk me out of it as push me on my motives. Maybe he saw something in me that made him worry, I don't know. I admitted that I didn't know for sure if I'd go through with it, and promised I'd drop out before the end if the going got too tough. That seemed to reassure him.

'Seminary was a mixed bag. Patches of aching loneliness amongst others of fantastic community life. I remember long nights of agonizing over whether to masturbate or not, and then feeling absolutely shattered because I'd given in once again. There were days when I thought the whole place was the most repressive, antiquated institution in the entire universe. And yet sometimes in morning prayer, or over the lunch table, or in a lecture from one of the crusty old teachers, there was a warmth and light and hope which made me as happy as I've ever been. I was in love with God, and that compensated for a lot of faults I could see in the church. Seminary was a crucible of human feelings — fear, faith, sexuality, cruelty and compassion all living alongside each other.

'I could've got out at any time. In fact they would have happily encouraged me out if they thought I wasn't up to it, despite the shortage of priests. Whether I was cut out for it; that was the main question which kept coming back to me in the night. I knew I wanted it. I wanted to be up the front with the cassock, and working the magic for people. But could I stand the pressures? Poverty, chastity, obedience – three wounds to bear for life. In the end you become part of a process with an inevitable end, and you lose your doubts in the palliative of routine. I wasn't brave enough to choose against the flow of events which led me all the way to ordination.

'People have the idea that religious life is full of direct communication from God, and some secret knowledge that others don't have access to. But it's not like that at all. It's all very ordinary. Preparing for the priesthood is like training to be a doctor or something – somewhere along the way you lose the awe for the healing process in amongst a mass of detail which has to be absorbed and regurgitated. Eventually you're not sure whether you believe something or whether you've simply memorized it for the sake of examinations. By the time I'd finished, I'd lost all perspective on my own faith. Being ordained was a leap in the dark – a jump of faith for the sake of faith.

'I ended up in St Joseph's parish in New Plymouth, on the West Coast of the North Island. It was a typical middle-class Catholic congregation. They liked me because I was young, and the

Those who marry God can become domesticated too – it's just as humdrum a marriage as all the others.
Graham Greene

homilies were short. I took to the life reasonably well. Saying mass was very special. Raising the host to heaven would bring tears to my eyes. There were parts of the life I didn't enjoy, and every parish has its internal politics. But by and large it suited me well, and all my doubts and qualifications went out the window. I was a priest, and that was what I was happy to stay. My bishop was well pleased with the start I'd made.

'It was a couple of months after I'd started there, and one of the parish families had invited me round for dinner. They had the typical large Catholic family – six children. Most of them I'd met at church, but the oldest daughter, Belinda, had never been. She was twenty-three, and making her own decisions in life. I thought she was drop-dead beautiful, even if priests aren't supposed to notice such things. She was full of life, and when we got into a discussion about theology later on, Belinda had firm views based on wide reading. Her parents worried at her absence from church, so they were pleased when she started attending again after that night. And naturally enough I was happy to see her there, thinking that I'd won her round by the force of my arguments.

'She made an appointment to see me. It turned out she wanted to have Confession, but she wasn't sure what she should be confessing and what she shouldn't. There were some things that the Church considered sins which she didn't, and she wanted to talk about them with me. We had a fantastic conversation, sparking off each other.

Even on issues which we disagreed strongly about, there was respect for the intellectual candour of the discussion. I came away enlivened, and we agreed to talk further. I told myself it was instruction in the faith. It was the first of many sessions. Sometimes we'd meet in a café instead of the presbytery, which was easier for her to get to from work. All of this was leading up to the sacrament of Reconciliation, and finally Belinda felt ready for it.

'We met in the church, though not in a booth. It was while pronouncing the prayer of absolution that I placed my hands on her head. And as I finished, and was about to take them away, she reached up and placed her hands on mine. I got such a jolt, as if someone had kicked me in the side of the head. It's a very intimate moment, confession and absolution, and the barrier between spiritual and sexual intimacy is tissue thin. In that moment I recognized how I'd been fooling myself, and what the real reason for the excitement over our meetings was. She looked up at me and I looked at her, and in that instant my whole future lay open before me. I knew what was happening, and what I had to do, and why I didn't want to do it.

'She drew my hands down and kissed them, watching me all the time. It was my call to make. I was the priest. I was the one with the power, the one who should know what was happening and stop it. But I didn't want to. That was it right there, in that moment. The sensation of being

> The only way to get rid of temptation is to yield to it. Resist it, and your soul grows sick with longing for the things it has forbidden to itself.
> Oscar Wilde

touched was stronger than my entire call to the priesthood. I *wanted* to be caressed and loved. What happened afterwards was just the consequences of the one instant of choosing. It was like a match amidst dry timber. The only thing I feel proud about in the whole experience was that I never tried to justify it to myself. I never pretended that it was anything other than what it was. After the first week I knew my priesthood was over.

'Apart from anything else, I was hopelessly in love. The first Sunday after it happened, when I raised the host, all I could see was Belinda's face, and I got an erection. The bishop offered all sorts of things. He would have moved me quite happily, given me a new start, sent me to another country to study. But I simply wanted to be with her all the time. So my priesthood was over almost as soon as it had started. All those years of training gone like smoke. But at the time I hardly even noticed. I thought of nothing but Belinda, and the future we would have together.

'It never occurred to me that things might change. I remember seeing a shadow of disappointment in her eyes when I told her I was leaving the priesthood. I'd expected her to be excited, naturally, seeing I was doing it for her. But something shifted after that. Her family was down on her like a ton of bricks. And it seemed to me she became a little contemptuous of me. Perhaps the unattainable had suddenly become available, and lost its attraction. We moved in

You have to accept the fact that part of the sizzle of sex comes from the danger of sex. You can be overpowered.
Camille Paglia

together, planning to get married, but things began to fall apart. And then one day I woke up and she was gone. There was a letter, which I burned without reading.

'So I gambled and lost everything. I spent a year feeling desperately sorry for myself. After a time the pain grew less sharp, and I began to get interested in life again. I did some retraining, headed overseas, and here I am. A failed priest. I'm sorry if I haven't been entirely honest with you. It tends to put people off, that's all. People are nervous enough around a priest, let alone a compromised one. I've tried hard to find some identity of my own; to just be John. For the first time ever, I think it's been happening here. I suppose it had to come out sooner or later.'

> There are few things more dreadful than dealing with a man who knows he is going under, in his own eyes, and in the eyes of others. Nothing can help that man.
>
> James Baldwin

Claire is carefully examining her wristwatch, toying with the winder on its side. She is having trouble making sense of the patterns.

There has been no scraping of cutlery on plates for some time. No work for jaw muscles, which seem universally relaxed. Siobhàn begins to laugh.

'What?' asks John, confused.

'Nothing, nothing. Only it's a first for me. Oh god, sorry. Sorry, Claire,' and she's away giggling again.

'I knew there was something, I just knew it,' Quentin congratulates himself. 'It's the way you hold your hands when you're talking. And that business about praying.'

'Here we are, rabbiting on about moral issues,

all the time sharing the table with a Catholic bloody priest,' complains Tasha.

'An ex-priest,' John corrects. 'It was four years ago now.'

'Nothing else you want to tell us, is there?' rejoins Tasha. 'You don't rip the heads off babies or howl at the moon Sunday evenings?'

'Are you all right, Claire?' asks John.

She looks up at him, wipes her nose with the back of her hand, shakes her head and looks down again.

> There are things to confess that enrich the world, and things that need not be said.
>
> Joni Mitchell

'Well,' decides Quentin, 'this takes us into new territory altogether. I hope you're not on some secret campaign to convert us all.'

'I'm me. The only thing that's changed is you've learned a little more of my history. It's not like I've been hiding things from you, or pretending to be something that I'm not.'

'How can you say that?' asks Claire, with a catch in her voice.

> I'm a liar, but an honest one.
>
> Federico Fellini

'I mean I haven't hidden who I am. Just because I used to be a priest once doesn't make me any less or more of a person. There's bits about all of us we haven't told to each other for one reason or another.'

'It's a largish bit you're talking about,' laughs Siobhàn. 'You might have given us some hint.'

'I suppose I haven't trusted you all enough until tonight. Look, I'm only an ex-priest, not an alien.'

'I'm not sure which is stranger,' muses Tasha.

'How about God, then?' asks Siobhàn. 'You said you gave up on the priesthood, but how about God?'

'Ask me an easy one, why don't you? No, I haven't given up on God, I don't think. There are times when I wonder if I had any choice about believing – maybe it just came with the genetic package like the colour of my eyes. And for a long time after I left the priesthood I felt that I'd been conned; conned into joining up and conned again into leaving. I wondered what the point of the whole thing was. I threatened myself with giving up the faith. And then I worked out that it wasn't a case of disbelieving in God; it was just that I was angry with God. If I gave up on God I wouldn't have anyone to be angry at, and that seemed a waste. I still don't understand what the whole exercise was about. But I've stopped worrying that I don't understand.'

'Religious horseshit,' pronounces Quentin. 'Mystical mumbo jumbo. God's supposed to be good and controlling the world and all that, but as soon as something comes up which suggests otherwise, all the little Christians say it doesn't matter; that it's the mystery of faith or some such crock. You can't have it both ways.'

'I wasn't trying to convince anyone,' John answers quietly. 'I was just trying to explain my own mixed-up point of view. You don't need to tell me it doesn't make sense.'

'But doesn't that make a nonsense out of your faith?' joins in Tasha. 'That's always been my

> May it not be that, just as we have to have faith in him, God has to have faith in us and, considering the history of the human race so far, may it not be that 'faith' is even more difficult for him than it is for us?
> W.H. Auden

> Religion to me has always been the wound, not the bandage.
> Dennis Potter

objection to religion; it becomes an irrational prop for people who don't want to face life and can't let go of their hope for a cosmic father-figure.'

'You could be right,' admits John. 'I'm not the best at defending the idea of God.'

'Come on, don't give in that easily, you big wimp!' encourages Siobhàn. 'It must mean something to you if you can give up so much of your life for it.'

'It means everything to me, or most things anyway. If I sound uncommitted, it's because I've never been very good on the *idea* of God. I can't conceive of the world without God, no matter how hard I try. We might as well talk about reasons why Quentin doesn't exist: some of them might be very good, and intellectually compelling. But in the end I'd have to say, "Hey, isn't that Quentin sitting next to us over there?" It seems stupid debating the existence of someone you know.'

'But that's just arrogance,' argues Tasha. 'You're cutting the ground out from under our feet. You're saying that no argument we can put up will ever convince you otherwise, because you have access to some other means of knowing that's not open to scrutiny.'

'I'm sorry if it comes across as arrogance. I suppose it does sound that way. But I'm not trying to convince you of anything. I'm only trying to explain how it is that I go on believing in God when there's so much evidence to the

> I rarely speak about God. To God, yes. I protest against him. I shout at him. But to open a discourse about the qualities of God, about the problems that God imposes, theodicy, no. And yet he is there, in silence, in filigree.
>
> Elie Wiesel

contrary. Faith is indefensible at the best of times. I wouldn't have talked about it if the subject hadn't come up.'

'There's plenty who seem to want to talk about it,' sneers Quentin. 'I can hardly get up the High Street without being stopped by some fundamentalist who wants to tell me I'm a sinner.'

'I get it as well,' acknowledges John. 'I can't help them. I feel no more kinship with them than you might have done with Maggie Thatcher when she was killing Argentinians. They're the religious equivalent of mosquitoes. But I've worked out how to get them off my back. I look them in the eye and say, "Why are you telling me this? Don't you know I'm God?"'

'The dessert is lovely,' Claire asserts bravely. The combination of caramelized bananas and fresh cream provides a safe reference point. John looks up at her in pleading, but she refuses to meet his gaze.

'Holy shit,' exhales Siobhàn, 'an ex-priest.'

'Let's not start on that again,' implores John. 'What's your view on God, Siobhàn?'

'I'm for him, most of the time, except for when I'm not. For sure, I believe in God all right. I'm just not sure if God believes in me, you know what I mean? Which is by way of saying that I don't know what difference it makes that I believe. To be honest, I don't give a toss about whether I'm saved or not. I do my best with what I've got, and if at the end of it all God wants to put me in

> **Fervour is the weapon of choice of the impotent.**
> Frantz Fanon

a torture chamber for doing it, then I'll say "Fook you" and find a place next to the rest of the Irish.'

'Why is it that so many people imagine God like a sadistic monster?' John ponders.

'Maybe it's their experience of life; the way it always turns to shit just when you think it's getting better,' suggests Siobhàn. 'Have you seen that Gary Larson cartoon? The one with God sitting up in heaven watching people on a screen, and with his finger poised over the "Smite" button? That's the way it seems to me sometimes. Mind you, I was helped along by all those priest friends of yours telling me that any time I started enjoying myself, God was waiting around the corner with a big stick to beat me up.'

'It's all mind control,' says Quentin. 'A way of keeping people in order. You give them the idea that there's a judge on the inside of their head, who sees everything they do. That way they're too nervous to get into trouble even when they think they can get away with it. It's an internalized father figure, who just happens to reinforce the values of society. I can't believe there are grown-up people who still go along with the idea.'

'There's this story that Carl Jung tells,' responds John. 'He was a young man, daydreaming. He sees this picture of a perfect day. The sky is blue, the sun's shining, all's well with the world. In the centre of the village there is a church, with all the good religious people coming and going. And high above the church, in the sky, is God presiding over it all. Then, in the middle of his daydream, Jung begins to see something which he can't bear to allow into his imagination. He switches off from his meditating in terror. For several days he goes around in a panic, exerting all his psychic energy in keeping out the terrible vision which is crouching at the edge of his consciousness. Eventually he can't stand the pressure any longer, and he allows the dream to flow again. There's the perfect day, the blue sky, the sun shining, and God presiding over the church. All is lovely. And then, as he watches, God excretes a great turd, which falls from the sky and smashes the church into little pieces.'

Even Claire has trouble restraining herself from laughter. Siobhàn is giggling uncontrollably.

'And the point of this is?' Quentin wants to know.

'Jung was the son of a pastor. He grew up detesting what he saw of church life. But after having that daydream, he was able to separate out the idea of God from the things that the church and religious people did.'

A church which has lost its memory is in a sad state of senility.
Henry Chadwick

'I remember one time at school when there was a teacher I hated,' recounts Siobhàn. 'She was a cow, Sister Veronica. I started a rumour that she'd been heading off into the storeroom with the caretaker during lunchtimes. I'd seen her go in there to read, so I knew it would raise some questions. The story got a bit out of hand, and before you knew, there were kids who swore they'd seen her being humped through the windows. It was like a dark shadow came over the school, and there were whisperings everywhere. In the end she was transferred to another place. I felt triumphant, but deep down I felt sick as well, knowing what I'd done to her.

'It got worse and worse. In the end I went down to the church to go to confession. I was sitting in the church, waiting for the booth to be free, and wondering how I could tell the priest and yet disguise it enough so's I didn't get in trouble. There was something strange came over me. It was like I could see Sister Veronica, and the way she was hurting. She was kneeling on her own, crying, and behind her there was this big crucifix, and there were tears in Jesus' eyes as well. I could feel this raw pain that was almost unbearable. I whispered, "I'm sorry," but it sounded so pathetic. And then both sets of eyes turned to me, and I felt such a sense of overwhelming love that I almost fell over. It was as if my Da was just holding me and hugging me, and I would be warm and safe for evermore.

'The priest came out of the booth and found me sobbing my heart out. I was a complete wreck. He never said a word. He just knelt down beside me and started praying alongside me. Later on when I got it together again, I said to him that I'd come down for confession. But he smiled and told me he thought it might not be necessary now.'

'I wish I knew what you were talking about,' reflects Tasha. 'I hear those sorts of stories and

'To forgive oneself'? No, that doesn't work: we have to be forgiven.

Dag Hammarskjöld

224

it's like people are from a different planet that I've never visited. The only way I can handle that sort of stuff is to think of it in psychological terms.'

'How d'you mean?' asks Siobhàn.

'You were under stress psychologically, and so there's some sort of internal balancing mechanism that cuts in to reassure you and stop you flipping out totally.'

'I guess,' tenders John, 'that the only issue is whether the mechanism is psychological or spiritual.'

'Don't get me wrong,' Tasha explains, 'there are times when I wish I could believe more. Talking about death and dying makes me wish I could get hold of something more substantial. I admire people who have faith in things they can't see, and feel somewhat jealous of them. But I can't get beyond my cynicism. It's how I've survived in life, and I can't let go of it to save myself.'

'Trust is hard to come by,' agrees John. 'It seems a kind of foolishness in today's world. But I don't think faith means you have to be a complete bloody idiot.'

'Perhaps you could be our flat-priest,' suggests Quentin. 'You could interpret the mysteries of life as they affect the five of us.'

My faith is a great weight hung on a small wire.
Anne Sexton

'When you think about it,' contributes Claire, 'God's at the bottom of everything we've been talking about.'

'I beg your pardon?' replies Quentin, in mock puzzlement.

'Everything we've been discussing since we started these dinners, it's all been about what's right or wrong, or how to live, or what happens when you die. They're all religious questions really, aren't they?'

'Only in the sense that everything about life is religious,' responds Quentin. 'Which makes your statement something of a tautology.'

'Don't be silly, Quentin. You can play with words as much as you like, but underlying all our issues is the question of what life's about. Whether or not life has a purpose, whether we're created or just some chance rearrangement of cells, whether there's such a thing as right or wrong: they're all ways of asking the same question. Is there a God or not?'

'Not,' asserts Quentin.

'That's fine, everyone has to work it out for themselves. But I don't think it's fair to suggest that anyone who has faith is brainless or naïve. Or that God is some sort of psychological crutch for people who aren't emotionally mature. And anyway, I'm not as convinced of your atheism as you are.'

'Meaning?'

'You might say you don't believe in God, but that's not the way you live. You're kind, you're sensitive, you try to do the right thing, you appreciate beauty, you believe in the future…'

'But for god's sake, Claire, religious people don't have a monopoly on those qualities. It's typical bloody Christian arrogance to be surprised

God hears no more than the heart speaks; and if the heart be dumb, God will certainly be deaf.

Thomas Brooks

The fruit of the Spirit is love, joy, peace, patience, kindness, generosity, faithfulness, gentleness and self-control. There is no law against such things.

The Bible

when ordinary heathen people exhibit signs of humanity or love.'

'I wonder,' breaks in John, 'if what Claire is saying is that there's a lack of grounding for right and wrong if there's no ultimate foundation...'

'John!' explodes Claire. 'I'm quite capable of sticking up for myself, thank you just the same. And that's not what I'm saying at all. I'm not interested in philosophical discussions about morality or theology. I'm talking about life and living. About what you do with pain, and how you keep hope and love alive when nobody seems to want them anymore. Of course life is terrible. We've all been hurt on the way through. But why keep on with it? Why is it that we keep searching for love when so much around us denies its existence? For me it's because I know that underneath it all, there *is* Love, and that it's able to be found. And I'm sure that deep intuition is within all of us, no matter how much we might deny it. We're all hungry for God, but we keep filling the hunger with other things.

'And while I'm speaking, I might as well say that I'm pissed off to find I've been sleeping with a bloody priest, who didn't even have the gumption to tell me. And that's why I'm bloody well crying, and if anyone offers me sympathy I'll kill them!'

'Perhaps,' suggests Tasha, 'this might be a good time for coffee?'

'I'm sorry, Claire, I didn't mean to hurt you,' says Quentin. 'I honestly don't know if I believe in

Our hearts are restless until they find their rest in thee.
Augustine of Hippo

God or not. I just can't stand the small-mindedness of people who seem to have everything wrapped in one package, with all the answers. It makes me want to attack. But there are times when I'm writing, and everything's coming in a rush so that I can't keep up with it, and I wonder afterwards where the stuff's coming from. I simply don't know. Believing in anything big or good seems such a contradiction in this world. I preserve my ability to love by erecting huge fences around it, and firing shots at anything that draws near. I don't know about God. God is too big to get a handle on. But this group of people – you people – I can feel something there. And even tonight, as much as I may knock it, Claire's faith and John's faith means something to me. It's like a bonfire in the night. Maybe I can't light one myself, but I can come and stand in the light and warmth for a while, and I like it there.

'If God meant anything at all to me, it'd be something to do with love. In those few moments in my life when I've been capable of real love, as opposed to lust or projected self-interest, I've found it deeply spiritual, for want of a better term. As if my love was part of a greater current which was always flowing beneath the surface, and which I'd just tapped into for a while. I remember hearing in a church or a film or something that God is love. And I thought, yes, I can understand that. Love's outside of religion or morality; it's accessible. If it turned out that God was something like that, then even I might have a

228

place, I suppose. And here with you lot, it seems almost possible, you know?'

There's a sort of quietness which descends upon them. John has moved to be close to Claire, and is stroking her hair. Tasha is hiding somewhere behind her eyes. Siobhàn sighs heavily.

'There's something I'd like us all to do, before we lose this moment,' she says quietly. 'Can we just hold hands round the table for a moment, and be quiet? Just to humour me, come on.'

As old as time itself, there's a circle of people, hand in hand. There's the flickering of candlelight, gentling each of the faces. There's some eyelids closed in contemplation, and there's some bright eyeballs in which joy dances. There's a silence, as warm and thick as a city night. And is there something else? Someone else? Or is it just the way the curtain moves in the breeze?

Do not the most moving moments of our lives find us all without words?

Marcel Marceau

Chapter Twelve

John

It seems impossible to avoid hurting and deceiving people, even when you love them. I never thought of myself as keeping secrets, and yet I suppose I was. Even now, I'm not convinced that being completely open would have been any better. I look back on that night with fondness and longing. Despite what I lost, I wouldn't have wanted to change the way things happened.

I'm not sure if we keep secrets or whether we are secrets. I can't even imagine what it would mean to know another person totally. There are bits of ourselves which come out from time to time, and more so the greater the trust we find. But the well of mystery is inexhaustible, and each time you dip the bucket, it comes up brimming. I don't even know myself entirely. Perhaps it's only through other people that we begin to understand ourselves.

Certainly there's something deep within us which drives us to confess. When I look back on those nights we had around the dinner table, it's not the issues I remember, but the people. The gradual seeping out of personality like blood on a bandage, until we all became relaxed about each other's wounds. That's what my priesthood was; an unhealed wound. The reason I couldn't speak

No blame should attach to telling the truth. But it does, it does.

Anita Brookner

230

freely about it was because the pain was still fresh. And, to be honest, because I suspected it would complicate things too much. I was scared that people would relate to me differently if they knew. As it turned out, my fears were at least partly valid.

I sometimes feel my faith as a curse. I imagine it to be similar to the experience of someone in a wheelchair or with multiple sclerosis or something. You want people to relate to you just as you are. But they see the wheelchair or the dribble on your lip, and there's some sort of screen comes down. You see it in their eyes, and you can almost read the word 'cripple' taking shape in their brains. It's that way with Christian faith. I might as well have someone walking in front of me with a bell, warning 'Unclean! unclean!'

And yet my faith is part of me, a sort of benign cancer in the soul. There's no way of separating it out; no chance of removing it without excizing my being at the same time. So what do you do when there's something about who you are which causes offence to the people you love? You do your best to hide it. You pretend to be normal like they are. Except you always end up giving yourself away, because you're not normal in the same way as other people. You're marked, branded, diseased. Cursed with faith.

I think Claire might have been the person I could have loved and lived with all of my life. I've loved a few times now, and it's hard to compare one with another. But at the time, I always felt she was the one for me, as much as that can be true of anyone. Perhaps it was the sense of loss that made it seem that way, like with a musician who dies before they've developed their best work. Probably I'm simply being maudlin and romantic. Love is a feeling that comes and goes. When either of us had woken up to find it gone, we would have needed something stronger and deeper to see us through. I'll never know if we were capable of that sort of commitment.

I always remember her staring into the distance. It was easy to think she was empty-headed, and I admit that I did at first. But I came to learn that it was her way of preserving a kind of innocent beauty in a world which was far from beautiful. As if she were turning inward to contemplate a finer realm; preserving it on our behalf and occasionally giving us insights into it. I have no photos of Claire, but I carry an image in my memory banks, and in it she's always staring into that pool of tranquillity.

I'm left with sadness, but not regret. I've never seen the point of wishing that your life was other than it is. It would have come out sooner or later that I was a failed priest. If I'd told her right from the outset, she would never have got together with me. It would've been too much of a betrayal of her own sense of what's right and wrong. So in that sense I'm glad of my deceit. It bought me several magic nights to savour in the privacy of my imagination. It would be crass to regret love simply because it ended up being lost. Everything in life slips away just as you're beginning to hold it. There's no point in being bitter about it.

Of course I tried to persuade her that nothing had changed. That it made no difference. She said that it was my keeping secrets from her that made it impossible; that she wouldn't ever know in the future whether she could trust me or not. But it wasn't that at all, really. It was the thought of sleeping with a priest, even an ex. Claire too was cursed with faith. I understood it completely, even though we never talked about it. She was as kind as she could be, and I gave in too easily. There are times when you recognize that all the resources you have will still be insufficient to change the way things are.

It seems like more than eighteen months ago. And yet, in another way, that final dinner we had together is still so fresh it might have been last week. Holding hands in the candlelight, with all our wounds and contradictions, we were as close as it's possible for a group of people to be. It only lasted for a few moments, but it was like some unspeakably exquisite gift. These things never last. The past is eroded with every new torrent of experience. And now I find myself opening to new possibilities, daring again to dream and wonder. A little uncertain whether this may not be the most ludicrous option possible. Who would have imagined it? Life retains its prerogative of surprise.

Maybe all one can do is hope to end up with the right regrets.
Arthur Miller

Claire

When I locked up tonight, I walked across to the other side of the street and looked back. It still seems unreal. I look at the sign and it's if the shop belongs to someone else. I try to look at the window with a critical eye, but it's hopeless. I just want to smile and stop people in the street and tell them that I did that. That it's mine and it's lovely. Now that it's real, I think it's even better than I imagined it would be.

I catch myself being happy and feeling guilty about it. Strange how joy can come again after thinking it never would. In those dark days after John left and Miriam died, grief was my lover. I remember being thankful for winter with its darkness and cold, and resentful when the days began to lengthen. Sleep was my only refuge. I looked forward to unconsciousness; to the welcoming dark and its absence of pain. Such incredible weariness; as if I was dragging a huge black rock behind me wherever I went. Which I was, I guess.

In the first few weeks I was angry. Even at the funeral I found it hard to be sad. The only thing which pierced my numbness was rage. I wanted to pound on the coffin and scream at her. I found myself waking up in the night shouting out in the foulest language. What infuriated me most was the way she did it. Because she'd jumped, we couldn't even see her body. They'd had to more or less shovel the bits together, and when the funeral director's assistant used the word 'remains' I

> Pain hardens, and great pain hardens greatly, whatever the comforters say, and suffering does not ennoble, though it may occasionally lend a certain rigid dignity of manner to the suffering frame.
>
> A.S. Byatt

234

wanted to punch her. It was a long time afterwards that I first cried in sorrow.

I don't think I was even aware that John was at the funeral until after it was almost over. You get caught up in the events, and you hardly even register people. And I was focused on Mummy and Daddy, and getting them through it. When he came up to me, his face seemed to be floating through the mist; a half-remembered ship from a distant port. He was lovely. He didn't try to say anything; he just held me. It's the one real memory I have from the day, the one event that's not surreal. I could have stayed there for ever, in his arms. Except I couldn't. He was gone as well, just like Miriam. And you can't hold the dead.

I loved him. In those early days I was sure we were going to marry, and I would have been happy with it. He had a strange mixture of anger and tenderness, and he could always make me laugh. I knew there was something special about him, but I never would have guessed. If only he'd been honest with me from the beginning, perhaps we could have made it work. But possibly not. Catholicism is such a strong force – it would have been a cross-cultural marriage. I never could have explained it to my parents.

He was a good man. Probably still is, though we've somewhat lost touch, apart from this invitation. I was thinking of him earlier today, in the midst of dressing a mannequin. There was always a hint of something tragic in his eyes. Even when I was telling him that it was all over, he

Love is a naked child: do you think he has pockets for money?
Ovid

seemed to lie down and take it like a dog which has been beaten too many times. Perhaps tragedy follows him around, though that's not a very good thought to be holding so close to the event. I wish him well, though I'm not over him enough to be able to pray for him yet.

Miriam's death was a watershed for us all. There I go, thinking of it in euphemisms again. It's like a family handicap, the way we can't use the word 'suicide'. As if by not mentioning it we might change the way it happened. But it did set us all free in a way. It was as if we'd all been engaged in some desperate attempt to stop her dying by the way we lived – as if it were up to us. And then when it happened we were all free to relax and get on with living. In my darker moments, I sometimes wonder if Miriam didn't sense that in us; that she was holding us back.

Now that the raw pain has subsided, I find times when I can almost be thankful for her life, with all its tragedy. She was wild and beautiful despite her madness. In some ways I wonder if she wasn't too passionate for life. The gleam in her eyes when she was really crazy was like the burning of a fire on the inside of her soul, which occasionally became too much to contain. It would spill over and sweep through our lives, making a mess of our careful order. Her death may have been her way of preserving her vision.

Mummy and Daddy almost didn't make it. They had the most terrible rows afterwards. I was sure they would divorce. But then they stopped

> Sometimes I wonder if suicides aren't in fact sad guardians of the meaning of life.
>
> Vaclav Havel

blaming and fighting, and sort of fell into each other's arms. They have a closeness borne out of shared pain that is deeper than any relationship I saw before. And Daddy is softer now. So much more accepting of me. I couldn't believe it when he offered to put up the money for the shop.

And so tonight I feel contented. I can see my shop across the road there, and it still looks wonderful. After darkness, light. Our scars never leave us, but the fresh hurt eases. And Quentin has been so good. I don't think there could be anyone better to share an apartment with. Though I miss those dinners we used to have. I wish that time had never ended.

> For us, the best time is always yesterday.
> Tatyana Tolstaya

Siobhàn

It took me a long time to forgive Claire. I couldn't believe she could be so prissy and bloody-minded as to give up on John. I would've had him on any terms. We would never have had to break up the flat if it hadn't been for that. That's the trouble with relationships; they get in the way of being friends. Not that I can talk, I suppose. It was me that first bedded John, and that before I even knew he was a bloody priest. But it wasn't like there was anything serious in it. Not like Claire and her storybook romantic scruples.

Looking back on that last night round the table, it got to me more than I thought. Something was going on there, more than we all knew. All that talk of death and God must have laid us bare. And that priggish bastard William, trying to make me responsible for his miserable little life. Thank God he survived. I might have had trouble shaking that one off. Anyway, all of that opened me up like a knife through butter. I felt more connected that night than I had for a long time.

I'm sure it was that got me started thinking of home. It was the same night that I dreamed about sitting around the family table at home, with the talk and the laughter flowing. After John said he was leaving we all felt desolate. We all knew we couldn't just go on without him. We'd touched something, reached a depth with each other that made it impossible to play at just being flatmates again. It would have been unbearable to be together with one of us missing, if you know what I mean. Better that we put an end to it properly.

It was simple but not easy to go back to Dublin. Everything was different, and most of it me. I was home, but I didn't belong there any more. Most of my friends were dead or married or gone. I was without work the first couple of weeks, and living at home. We nearly killed each other. Getting a place on my own was the best thing I ever did. I miss the people, you know, but I like my solitude as well.

People's not the only thing I miss, and all. I've not had sex a year or more; at least not with anyone but myself. I think all that talking about it in the flat robbed me of the pleasure. I found it harder to do it without thinking. And it's a hard thing to be thinking and screwing at the same

To know after absence the familiar street and road and village and house is to know again the satisfaction of home.

Hal Borland

Sex is the last refuge of the miserable.

Quentin Crisp

238

time. Not that it stopped me at first. For a few weeks after that thing with William, I was into bed with a different man every second night. And, what was her name? Beth, her and all. It was like pushing on a tooth that's aching — there's some weird satisfaction for a time in increasing the pain. And I wanted to punish men in general.

But moving meant I had to make some changes anyway. At first it was just the case that I wasn't getting any because I didn't know anyone and I couldn't be bothered. Only slowly it dawned on me that I was feeling clearer in my head. My dreams were not so tangled, and I began to feel a little less cynical about life. Still, I don't think anything would have changed if weren't for SLAA. It was Rachel at work who told me about it.

We'd been talking about men, and she'd been telling me the sort of mess she'd been getting herself into. Especially with lads who'd give her a hiding. She seemed to pick them without fail. And how this group she went to now had helped. When she told me the name of it, I nearly fell off my chair with the laughing. 'Sex and Love Addicts Anonymous', she said it was. I was keen on sex myself, but I'd never thought of it as something you could be addicted to.

She never pushed it, did Rachel, which was a good thing. It was only in those quiet nights, when I was on my own and looking out on the river, that I saw my life for what it was. Only then that I began to understand myself and why I was doing what I was doing. I knew then that

Our lives teach us who we are.
Salman Rushdie

there were two people within my skin. One who was loving and playful and fey, and another who was out to destroy everything the other built. And I could see my history — the way I'd been smashing whatever I cared about in order to keep it safe.

I understood for the first time that I was using sex as a weapon. So I talked to Rachel again, and went with her to a meeting. A part of me just wanted to run, it seemed so naff. But the women who were there were ordinary people like myself, and there was no hype. Women who'd been hurting and knew they had to change, and were helping each other to do it. The thing that sold me on it was that it had a spiritual base. Change meant working in partnership with your 'Higher Power', whatever you understood that to be.

That was the most surprising gift out of the whole thing. That sense of connection with something bigger than yourself. I came to recognize that it was the spiritual side of my life which I'd been neglecting, and it was that which was wreaking havoc in me. I feel like I have some sort of centre now, which means I can go into relationships without desperation. I haven't been 'saved', and I'm not a zealot. But I'm quietly optimistic, and my life is so much better than it was.

It's a shame this wedding is too far away for us all to get together again. Perhaps it's better that we don't. There's nothing like going back to shatter illusions.

Quentin

Today was one of those days. The first thing I opened in the mail was a rejection slip for a short story. I could feel the depression settling like a fog, despite myself. And then the other envelope I opened was an acceptance for my novel! There is nothing in life to match the exhilaration that this sort of news brings. I can hardly wait for Claire to get home to have someone to share it with.

It was especially significant because yesterday was my third birthday. Which is to say, it's three years to the day that I learned I was HIV positive. Every day of life is a bonus; every year a miracle which I'm grateful to be able to celebrate. And now, to know that I'll realize the dream of being a published novelist is almost too sweet to know what to do with. Why is it that the high points of life are more difficult than the low points?

It was bizarre of course that it ended up being John's secret which broke apart our flat (I wanted to write community, but it was hardly that). And all the time I was nursing the mother of them all. I imagine if we'd gone on much longer with our dinners, it would've come out. Luckily, John stole the limelight and I didn't need to face it. Not that it would have been too bad, I suspect. We seemed to find a profound level of acceptance and respect before it all fell apart.

Claire knew all along. I needed to tell someone, and I never could resist Claire. She's been so completely marvellous the whole way through, cheering me up and looking after me. And even

Men with secrets tend to be drawn to each other, not because they want to share what they know but because they need the company of the like-minded, the fellow afflicted.
Don DeLillo

now, I appreciate her being with me in this place more than I'm easily able to say. She wanted me to tell the others, and there were undoubtedly opportunities, but I was too cowardly. It takes me most of my energy to cope with the prospect of my own mortality.

And it was rather fun to keep everyone guessing about my sexuality. That was decided long ago, but I enjoyed maintaining an air of ambiguity. I committed myself to chastity after testing positive. Quite the little puritan. John would have been proud of me, had he known. My love for women was a way of channelling my submerged libido. Though to be honest, I always had an attraction to women; it just wasn't ever something I could consummate.

I stepped out of the gay scene to make it easier for me. I never could have maintained abstinence with the sort of life I lived before. It was also a way of hiding from the consequences of my illness. Attending funerals for past lovers is not the best way to keep a positive frame of mind. In some ways I've become a New Age monk. I lock myself up in my cell of writing, and observe the sacred walls of cynicism to keep unstained from the world.

Without the comfort of any belief, writing has taken on new significance for me. It's my version of eternal life. My words will live on after I've gone. They'll be my children to carry on my name. It's a legacy of sorts; though books are difficult to snuggle up to in the lonely watches of the night.

But this acceptance letter is a kind of rebirth for me — the first solid intimation of hope for too many years. I think only those who are dying can appreciate what that means.

I miss those dinners we shared together. One day, if I have enough days left, I'll write a book about them. They were high points for me. I don't suppose we ever decided much, or even agreed with each other. But there was a vitality in the talking; as if some of the issues actually *mattered*, and that our discussion of them could make some sort of difference to the way that each of us lived our lives. Too often we skate over the surface of life, taking it for granted and living with our petty compromises. I've reached the stage where I want to throw the doors open and shout at people to wake up. We're being smothered to death under clichés and instant TV dinners.

I had a great deal of respect for John. I don't suppose he ever would have known it, and I didn't do a great deal to enlighten him. But even when I was crying him down, he seemed to me to be one of those rare people with an uncomplicated heart. There was genuine goodness there; a little like Claire in that respect. Not that they could ever have survived together. Life would have had to take them apart, if only to prove that there's no such thing as happy endings.

He stunned us all with his confession. It caught me by surprise, even though I'd been expecting it. All my prejudices against the church rose up and began barking. I remember trying to apologize to

Most people, I'm convinced, don't think about life at all. They grab what they think they want and the subsequent consequences keep them busy in an endless chain till they're carried out feet first.
Philip Larkin

him later on, but I don't think he was interested. By then he was consumed with the knowledge that it was over between him and Claire. If ever there was a person to make me think there might be something in religion, it would be John. There's Claire, but I've always thought that her faith was a function of her kindness, rather than the other way round. John had enough devil in him to have other options.

But these are days of celebration, not nostalgia. I've prepared a little food for us to dream over.

Tasha

I'm not sure which is the greatest distance – time or miles. Either way I'm so far away now from where I was back then. It's hard to reconcile my life before and my life now. I have to think hard to remember the connecting links. It was John's revelations that did it for all of us, but more for me than most. I can't recall much of what we said to each other, but I remember vividly those last few moments holding hands around the table. It was spooky. We all knew that something was moving, even though we weren't sure what it was.

When John left, it gave me the excuse I'd been looking for to get a place on my own. It was hard saying goodbye, but exciting at the same time. My stoic side makes me rush over emotions anyway. Judith's death hit me harder than I'd anticipated. We got very close before the end, when I was visiting her in the hospice once a week. I always wanted to bring her something better than grapes, but I didn't have anything else. She understood. I often thought it was her comforting me rather than the other way round. Until the end, when the morphine started to take over.

John came to the funeral. I was caught by surprise. I'd let the others know, but I couldn't find a contact number for John in time. I've never asked him how he came to be there — whether it was seeing it in the paper or whether he heard from one of the others. Anyway, it was lovely to see him there. We would have had all of us together, except that Claire was still recovering from her sister's death, and couldn't face another funeral.

I'd already taken over Judith's job, and it seemed to work out well. I crossed swords with a few in the department, but once we understood where the boundaries were, everyone settled down and got on with it. It blew me away to find out that Judith had left me a diamond necklace in her will. It's not the sort of thing I find much use for, but I'll be wearing it tomorrow. So in some senses at least, she'll be with me. I'm not sure what she'd make of all this.

And then my mother dying so soon afterwards. I found it difficult to live with myself when it first occurred to me that I felt more for Judith than for my mother. But why shouldn't I? Judith had done more for me. Neither of the boys was at the funeral, and I was glad. I did manage to cry, though more for what had happened to us all out of grief. And then there was John again,

> **No one's death comes to pass without making some impression, and those close to the deceased inherit part of the liberated soul and become richer in their humanness.**
>
> Hermann Broch

throwing his arms around me. I couldn't believe it. I said something stupid about having to stop meeting that way.

We went for a coffee afterwards. He was great. He just sat and listened while it all poured out. Maybe it's a skill he learned when he was a priest or something. I don't know when I've ever talked at that length or depth before. I felt very safe, and I have to admit it cleared my head afterwards. It was a couple of days later that I decided I was going to travel. I had a letter from Tim in Australia, asking me again to come and visit. This time I rang him and told him I was going to do it. There was nothing left to hold me.

Moving to the Southern Hemisphere was like taking the lid off my spirit. It was certainly much more than a geographical shift. I feel physically lighter, as if there's less gravity on this side of the world. What I think is more likely is that I left behind a great weight of resentment, like a caterpillar shedding its cocoon. My cynicism got bleached in the sun, I suspect. I've become altogether more trusting, hopeful and vulnerable. For the first time ever, I don't feel as if I'm battling against the odds.

I've begun to be interested in the spiritual side of life. I suspect it was our discussions which sparked it all off, but it's been a long time until I've been able to overcome my disbelief. Now I find myself doing something remarkably close to praying from time to time. I think I listen to other people a great deal more than I used to. I've come to appreciate the natural world and be thankful for it; something which would never have occurred to me in my previous incarnation.

And now all this. It seems too bizarre to believe. No amount of going over the details makes sense of it. It happened, and I suppose that's all that matters in the end. And tomorrow there will be no going back.

John wakes with the sharp slices of sunlight piercing the room. He breathes deeply in that pre-conscious contentment, and knows that the air in his nostrils is the air of home. The sky outside is the high blue Antipodean dome, and the birds rejoicing in it are undoubtedly the birds of New Zealand.

It is natural on this day that his thoughts should return to that other bedroom on the far side of the world. And more specifically to that table, around which so much took place. He once again pauses to be thankful. So much and so far. He reaches down to find the letter from Claire, which he'd read before sleep. The words are unchanged, and once again he smiles as he scans it. It's the last paragraph which holds his attention.

Gratitude unlocks the fullness of life. It turns what we have into enough, and more. It turns denial into acceptance, chaos to order, confusion to clarity. It can turn a meal into a feast, a house into a home, a stranger into a friend. Gratitude makes sense of our past, brings peace for today, and creates a vision for tomorrow.

Melody Beattie

And so, John, I wanted once again to thank you for the times we shared together, and your consideration of my feelings when it became impossible for us to continue. As will be evident from what I've written above, I'm very happy now; as happy as I can ever remember having been.

It never ceases to amaze me how happiness can rise from the ashes of tragedy. I suppose if my faith were stronger, I might expect it to happen more often. But you'll know all about that, and out of all that has gone before has come this wonderful event. So my happiness I wish for you. Quentin is leaning over my shoulder and agreeing, and I know he's written separately. It's the most special of days, and I wish I was there to celebrate it with you. We join in sending you and Tasha our deepest love, and a wonderful life together. And don't spend your honeymoon talking!

> That which is endless
> has no end.
>
> Quentin

....

Alt.spirit@metro.m3
Alternative spirituality for the third millennium

Mike Riddell

Life is so busy, so noisy, there's so much stuff
to get through, so many things to keep up with.
How can anyone make sense of it all? In this
book, Mike Riddell tries to explore some of
the possible meanings in the things that happen
to us. And so these are his rants and raves
about an assortment of subjects from risk to
technosurfing, from dreaming to sexuality.

Weaving its way through them is the love
story of two ordinary mixed-up urbanites,
Generation Xers. Vincent has a mindless job in a
bank, Marilyn works mindlessly as a prostitute.
Can they get it together in their search for more
meaningful lives?

ISBN 0 7459 3711 X

All Lion books are available from your local bookshop, or can be ordered direct from Lion Publishing. For a free catalogue, showing the complete list of titles available, please contact:

Customer Services Department
Lion Publishing plc
Peter's Way
Sandy Lane West
Oxford OX4 5HG

Tel: (01865) 747550
Fax: (01865) 715152